For Joyce & Holt x2,

ENJOY THE HOLLYWOOD
Humor — FOLLOW YOUR
DREAMS!

BLESSINGS,

OPEN-FIELD RUNNING

OPEN-FIELD RUNNING

The Adventure
of Selling a
Screenplay
(A Memoir)

BRAD CATHERMAN

SEABOARD PRESS

JAMES A. ROCK & COMPANY, PUBLISHERS

Open-field Running: The Adventure of Selling a Screenplay (A Memoir)
by Brad Catherman

SEABOARD PRESS

is an imprint of JAMES A. ROCK & CO., PUBLISHERS

Address comments and inquiries to:
SEABOARD PRESS
9710 Traville Gateway Drive, #305
Rockville, MD 20850

E-mail:
jrock@rockpublishing.com   lrock@rockpublishing.com
Internet URL: www.rockpublishing.com

Trade Hardcover ISBN: 978-1-59663-567-8

Library of Congress Control Number: 2007924147

Printed in the United States of America

First Edition: 2007

This memoir is for

Mom
for encouraging me
to use my imagination

Dad
for teaching me
about handling adversity

son Andy
for reminding me
to look at the world with wonder

brother Gary
for his unconditional love

Screenplays and
screenwriting awards of Brad Catherman

North Wind — Viking Chieftain avenges the murder of his parents by an evil warlord, and later converts to Christianity through an enslaved monk. Historically accurate. In development with Loyola Productions. A Quarter-Finalist in The Writers Network Competition.

Spec screenplays available

Wheels — Romantic comedy about an able-bodied hubcap tycoon who is sentenced to live for one year in a wheelchair for violating his city's handicapped parking ordinance; learns about love and the important things in life. Winner of Finalist Awards at the New Century Writer, Charleston International Film Festival, and American Screenwriters Association competitions, plus a Quarter-Finalist in The Writers Network Competition.

Scattered Seeds — Based-on-fact Civil War story of 400 Southern women and children shipped north from Roswell, Georgia, by General Sherman to work-camps and prisons. Received Honorable Mention in the Skorpeonyx Screenplay Search Competition.

Cleaning Up — Musical comedy about a young, white entertainment lawyer who "discovers" talented black maid, followed by their special relationship.

CATV — Based-on-fact murder mystery in city cable television franchise political fight in early 1980s.

Brothers' Brunch — Traces the 45-year relationship of two brothers through sports, marriage, births, deaths, adultery, embezzlement, alcoholism, illness, and love of family.

Wings on High — Aging athlete gets a second chance to find peace late in life through help of an angel.

FOREWORD

This ain't the half of it. If I had to tell the *whole* story of my first screenplay deal in all of its detail, and how this book came about, there would be twice as many pages. For the person seeking ideas to break into the movie-making business, no amount of detail is too small and I trust some particulars in this book serve that end. To the reader simply wanting to be entertained with some of the behind-the-scenes goings-on of a wannabe screenwriter, I hope I have met that objective. But beware, all: the reader may begin to share my sense of frustration from the dead-ends, missed opportunities, confusion, rejection and zaniness of the inexact science of selling a screenplay, all while I tried to maintain my sanity and keep a day job. The author found solace in being able to laugh, mostly at himself, and urges readers to consider this option when faced with their own impossible dream.

If I had to list and thank all of the people whose help and passion pushed me along, this book would be much, much larger, in fact, deserving of another book just to thank them all. Pattie Baker, Terry Cunningham, Jeff Kaufman, Tracy Arsenault, Kevin Knaus and J.D. Fite represent a host of steadfast friends who kept me energized down the homestretch. All of the teachers from my formal education, especially the early years, each deserve a chapter of praise no matter what marks they gave me.

Fr. Eddie Siebert and the great people at Loyola Productions became the heroes of my screenwriting career when they put one of my scripts into development — and I hope many more chapters to come are written for them. And blessings to Dr. Gil Watson and Northside United Methodist Church in Atlanta for all the blessings they sent my way.

Let me now extend a global thanks to those helpful but forgotten folks, including some people who never even knew I was a wannabe writer, but whose zest for life had a way of rubbing off on me. If the book misses the mark to convey a measure of humor and hopefulness in these pages, the blame is all mine.

Thanks. Sorry. I can't find a better word.

Chapter 1

The Field of Play

About six years ago, I was sitting alone in a fast food place, just daydreaming, passing some time. I noticed a family sitting nearby. It was a multi-generational gathering consisting of a grandmother, a mother and father, some children, and a teenage boy. While they were a few tables away, and spoke a mix of English and Spanish, I heard their story: the teenager had just received his driver's license, and I gathered that he had earned the money to buy the slightly damaged car parked beyond the window of the restaurant. Words fail me now in describing the level of love, joy, and pride that the family was sharing at that moment.

This experience became a gift and a warning to me, the writer, not to indulge too much in fantasy lest the real stuff of life around me escape unnoticed. People connect with the real emotions of life presented on the screen, even in stories as far from everyday experience as science fiction or flights of fantasy.

My musings that day in the restaurant came just after I had sold my first screenplay, on the night of my 46th birthday in 2001. I laughed to myself as I remembered an incident that had occurred along the rugged path leading up to that sale. Years before, I had called an agent who had loved this particular script, the one I had just sold. He had liked the synopsis enough that I sent him the completed, full-length version. Soon thereafter I dutifully called to follow up. Upon hearing my name, his assistant put me through to him, immediately. The agent did not hesitate:

HIM: It was terrible. Especially the dialogue. Awful.
ME: Thanks for your … honesty.
HIM: I was going to write you a letter and somehow …
ME: … yes?
HIM: … break the news not so *bluntly*. It was very, very bad.
ME: Thanks for your … honesty.
HIM: Maybe someone will think differently than I do …

I've often wondered what the letter would have said.

It's not that I couldn't find people in the business who liked the script, it was that, invariably, I found people who liked the script but could do me no good. An independent producer (so independent that he didn't have any money, contacts, or experience) chimed in with this:

IND: We like your Viking script a lot!
ME: Thanks!
IND: Good dialogue! Great action! Good moral!
ME: Thanks!
IND: But, maybe we first do it as a stage play.
ME: Huh?
IND: A stage play. Off Broadway.
ME: How far off Broadway?
IND: Off-off.
ME: What about the scenes with the ocean and big fires?
IND: Well, that's a problem. Maybe lighting and sound
    effects …?
ME: So …
IND: We're a little undercapitalized at the moment.
ME: So …
IND: We'll get back to you. Soon.

It never happened.

During the 18 years since the first seed of passion was planted to write a screenplay, I had written eight other scripts, won awards in six screenwriting competitions, sold three script options (for $1 each), hired and fired four agents, and purchased four filing cabinets to hold all the rejection letters. Before I finally sold my first screenplay, I had received endorsements from a Catholic monastery and a United States Senator, survived two marriages and their divorces, lost a parent to cancer, overcame eight corporate downsizings, and became father to the greatest boy in the world.

During that 18 years I struggled to stay focused, and I never quit running. I couldn't do less.

Now, still in my revery, I got up and moved to the trash bin with my fast food tray, emptied it, and then reached into my pocket to retrieve a blue 3" x 5" index card on which was written my grocery list. Screenwriters always have lots of index cards. A smile found me as I remembered an incident that occurred a dozen years back. A woman in a grocery store, a stranger, standing behind me in the check-out line, lent me money when I didn't have enough to pay the total the cash register rung up. It was during a time when I was out of work—and I was so embarrassed and prideful that I didn't even ask for her name and address so I could repay her. In my grocery bag that day were the pen and index cards I used to outline the screenplay that became my first sale. Many times over the next decade, the thought of that woman— that Good Samaritan—kept me energized late at night, writing, finishing, so that I wouldn't let her down.

Chapter 2

Hey, I Can Do That!

In 1983, as an Account Executive with Home Box Office in the Atlanta Regional Office, my job was to go into local cable television systems and help develop marketing plans for HBO and Cinemax, so that, hopefully, more consumers would subscribe to our movie services than to those of the competition. I got paid to watch and learn about movies, too. Even though my formal cinematic training up until that time had been restricted to an introductory class in film at Emory University in the fall of 1978, as I watched I had the same ongoing thought that many people have every day, no matter what they do for a living: "Hey, I can do that!" Or, sometimes, the slightly more jaded version: "Boy, look at the junk they put on the screen, blah, blah, blah. Why won't they produce *my* screenplay (the one I might get around to writing someday)."

One day these reoccurring thoughts blossomed into action. I decided to take the next step: to actually write one. After all, I loved movies, and I *had* gotten an A in that course where we had learned to critique film technique and appreciate snappy dialogue. *How hard could it be?* But, a little research wouldn't hurt! The "bible" on the subject of screenwriting, said the guy at the book store, was Syd Field's *Screenplay*. "Same text that they use in film school," he promised.

After spending my ten bucks and an afternoon reading the 240-page book about building plots, three acts, and believable characters according to Mr. Field, I took his first piece of advice and purchased packs of 3" x 5" index cards. On about 150 cards, I wrote down scenes, dialogue and plots. Then, I turned on my JC Penney Smith-Corona Concord model 10 electric typewriter and cranked in a piece of paper. That first Saturday afternoon, after laboring for more than three hours, I counted the finished pages. Four. This wasn't as easy as I thought. But it sure was fun.

A screenplay is supposed to be about 120 pages, according to the book, or one minute of action for every page, to come up with a two hour movie. I always thought that this was a bogus rule, since action scenes written with such descriptions as "the battle raged on and on ..." could last several minutes on film. How could you time this?

After spending the next two months of free time on nights, weekends, holidays, and vacations, I finished my first script. The problem was it contained only 49 pages. OK, so it wasn't the right length, but I reasoned that I could market it as a "treatment," which is industry jargon for a script outline (or in my case, a script that was short for lack of more words to fill pages).

That first script was entitled *CATV* and dealt with the cable television industry (hence community antenna television, or *CATV*) in the late 1970s and early 1980s. The focus of the script was the factual backdrop of "cable TV franchising," the business practice of having several cable companies "bid" on the rights to wire a city. The City Council votes, and the majority determines whether a particular cabler will be allowed to sell service within the city limits. Shady and illegal "politicking" (bribes) landed some city officials and their "friends in business" in jail as FBI investigations netted some highly publicized arrests and convictions of this type of criminal.

I had watched the action from the sidelines as an employee of Cox Cable Communications in Atlanta. While none of the dirty deals took place there, my job gave me an "insiders" vantage point from which to follow the investigations and to read about them in the trade press. This period in business history came and went quickly but with such very high-profile consequences, I was convinced it could form the basis for a good movie.

Of course, having plunged in, I wanted to get some quick feedback on my work. There are a few well defined routes available for selling a script, including having it "repped" by an agent or in some cases (if you have clout) sending the script directly to a studio, producer, or actor. The Writers Guild publishes a list of agents who are "signatories," and specifically identifies those who are agreeable to reading scripts of "first time" (unknown, unproduced, wannabe) writers. Me.

I sent query letters to agents who were seeking new blood, and just to hedge my bets, also to agents not seeking new writers. To further hedge my bets, I also sent letters and occasionally my treatment to studios, writers, and actors directly. My rejection mail piled up daily, but the California postmarks were at least tangible evidence that I was moving. Maybe not moving forward, but at least moving.

While I was working for HBO, a high level executive pulled some strings and managed to submit my treatment for *CATV* to my employer. HBO "passed," and although they didn't give the reason, I couldn't blame them for rejecting a script which dealt with the dirty laundry of the cable operators—essentially, their customers.

During an HBO sales meeting one year, I was seated next to Michael Fuchs, the person most responsible for changing the way movies are financed and brought to cable. I'm amused today recalling my shyness in not wanting to press my screenplay ideas on him. What I remember most about that chance meeting was his wristwatch. Because he lived in New York and was doing most of his business in Los Angeles, he had one of those watches with two faces—one for east coast time and one for west coast time, three hours apart. I promised myself that one day I would wear one like it because I would need it.

While engaged in the early processes involved in pushing my first script, it occurred to me that perhaps refining the "product" would also be helpful. I responded to an advertisement in a film trade publication from Linda Seger, Ph.D. She was a "script doctor," an industry term for someone hired by the large studios and writers to critique and improve scripts. Her expertise was in helping to shape dialogue, characters, and action to meld them into better stories. She herself did no writing; she was more of a "script writer's therapist." I hired her from a distance, she in Los Angeles and I in Atlanta, for a few hundred dollars to critique *CATV*. I found her lessons by correspondence useful, although one time I became upset when she continued to confuse characters in the story. My script was better for her input; although, unfortunately, not a page longer. And, still not good enough to win her recommendation to agents or producers in the industry. She became too expensive for me to continue with her.

For a fleeting moment, I considered film graduate school. I would have lots of those fleeting moments, particularly on bad days at the office. But my corporate life had taken on a kind of fascinating "inertial momentum" of its own, and I enjoyed marketing. I had an undergraduate degree in psychology, and I approached marketing as a kind of behavioral modification therapy for the masses. The patients got well, so to speak, if they bought your product. Marriage, new suits, a mortgage, and a company car cemented the course of my life. The "golden handcuffs," I think they called it at the office. A "sell-out," some others might say.

I didn't write another word or try to find an agent, producer, script doctor, studio, or interested actor for the remaining six years of the 1980s, except for one failed attempt to win a position reserved for aspiring writers at the renowned Sundance Film Lab. Job changes, relocations, a house purchased, travel schedules, a house sold, a marriage failure, a stint at graduate business school, a second marriage, trying to stay in shape, cutting the grass, taking out the trash, and other of life's commitments commanded my time. But as Robert Redford, founder of the Sundance Film Institute, said in the movie *The Natural* when his character, Roy Hobbs, was asked why after not playing baseball for a period of sixteen years he was suddenly back in, "my mind was always on the game."

Mine, too.

Chapter 3

Take 2

It was New Year's Eve 1990. Now, the Beginning of a New Decade, which always intensifies the pressure to make New Year's resolutions that count. My New Decade Resolution was to reignite my passion for screenwriting. For years, I had asked myself the same question every New Year's Eve: "If not this year, then when?" This time the answer was "Now!"

The May 3, 1990, *Wall Street Journal* ran an article with the headline "Hunt for Blockbusters Has Big Movie Studios in a Spending Frenzy ... Cash-Flush Film Chiefs Need Projects, So Even Scripts Are Selling for $1 Million."

Fine by me.

While outlining more screenplays, I queried more agents about the first one without success. Was my Atlanta location sending the wrong message? Would no serious screenwriter live anywhere but Los Angeles? Or was it that, perish the thought, my script *CATV* wasn't good enough? (Naw.)

The rejection letters continued to pour in until I had to go buy another filing cabinet to contain them all. Those letters from agencies, studios, producers, directors, and actors either said "no thanks" or that "we are returning the script, or log line (brief two-sentence script description), unread because you *have to submit it through someone known to us, an agent or a lawyer*" (emphasis mine).

Since I wasn't being invited to any Hollywood parties, it wasn't likely I would know anybody who would be "known to us."

Linda Seger's script-doctoring career had continued to blossom. Her rate was then $2000 for "a very complete analysis of the strengths and problem areas, plus a page by page analysis." My car wasn't worth that much, and I certainly couldn't afford her. Was she worth that much? Her 2007 web site listed a script analysis fee of $3000 and many studio clients, so I suppose she continued to become a very valuable player in Hollywood. (My car still isn't worth that much.)

To become an agent, a full-fledged signatory of the Guild, did one need to obtain a license, say, as one would to practice dentistry? Or, was it slightly easier, say, like getting a driver's license? Did it require the requisite skill and knowledge for, say, getting a fishing license?

But could I use a "lawyer?" Any lawyer? A lawyer who is a signatory of the Writers Guild? Would a real estate lawyer do? A tax lawyer?

I knew a lawyer.

Jeff Lewis and I had played Little League Baseball together. Basically, he would either strike out or hit a home run, as I remember. Later, when I played football for Marist School in Atlanta, he played for rival Westminster. Basically, I would either run the football and gain some yardage or Jeff would kind of pick me up and slam me on my head, as I remember.

At the University of Georgia, Jeff was a linebacker and co-captain of the football team, along with being a lyric baritone and stage actor. After law school, he had roles in the movie *Free Jack*, NBC's *In the Heat of the Night*, and in Hallmark's *Caroline?* and *Decoration Day*. While a part-time actor, Jeff has successfully won landmark court rulings. He speaks fluent German (as a second language, I should note, for reasons which will become important later).

Our conversation went like this (in English):

ME: I need a lawyer to represent my scripts.
JEFF: I'm not an entertainment lawyer.
ME: It doesn't matter.
JEFF: What's the main qualification?
ME: Letterhead.
JEFF: OK, but it'll cost you postage and a commission.
ME: Sold!
JEFF: I haven't told you the commission rate yet.
ME: It doesn't matter.
JEFF: And you buy lunch.
ME: Sold!

I had my first agent! No matter what question anyone asked me, the response was the same: "Sorry, you have to ask my agent." It didn't matter if the question was "So, how about those Braves?" or "When are you going to take out the trash?" or "What do you want for dinner?" Same power answer every time. I was now a player!

Just as with marketing anything from soda pop to automobiles, I needed to create some "buzz." I knew it was going to take more than just sending out the script ... I needed some public relations. I needed some "heat," as they called it.

A friend who was a Creative Director at a promotion agency, Jeff Kaufman, had a movie poster designed showing some scenes from *CATV*. This would accompany and draw special attention to a mailing going out to 265 producers and studios. I couldn't afford to place an ad in *Variety* using the movie poster art. But I did send a press release to the major newspapers, magazines, and trade publications that connected my screen treatment to the controversy surrounding the cable television franchising process.

Only one newspaper called me and ran the story, the *Atlanta Journal*, on April 20, 1991. The headline screamed, "Screenplay

on Dirty Cable Deals," and went on to say, "Atlantan Brad
Catherman is shopping around a screenplay … about corruption
in the cable television industry . Replete with religious blackmail,
double-dealing spouses and political backstabbing …"

That would have been OK, but the article gave the story a
negative slant by stating, "Bet you won't see this one on cable
television anytime soon." While probably correct, the story was
linked to the fact that I was to start a new job as Director of Sales
Promotion for Turner Broadcasting the following week. So much
for the value of buzz.

I approached my new boss at Turner, Terry Cunningham, on
my first day, expecting it to be my last day, and showed him the
article. He assured me that Turner is a place that embraces "diverse, creative thinking" from its ranks, and not to worry. (Terry
had a script of his own.) I worked there for the next three years,
and my "hobby" was encouraged. Turner was a place where outside creative and recreational interests were always encouraged. It
was good for morale.

So, while I was still employed and able to pay the postage,
solicitations for *CATV* were mailed to the producers. Several studios replied asking to see the synopsis, essentially an outline of
several pages. One of those was Hemdale International, winner of
the Best Picture Oscar two years in a row for *Platoon* and *The Last
Emperor*. Maybe the movie poster had worked!

By reading the film trade press, I learned of a technique often
used by agents to create a sense of urgency: set a deadline for
studios to submit their written bids. A new letter was sent from
Jeff Lewis' law firm to the studios currently reading and evaluat-
ing *CATV*: "Please submit your bid, along with the terms and
conditions, by Friday, July 19, 1991 at 5:00 p.m. EST."

No bidders responded by the deadline.

I spent the next few months rewriting *CATV*. It was over 100
pages by fall. Perhaps this new version would trigger renewed in-

terest on the part of the producers? A new "bid deadline" was set for January, 1992, for those producers who expressed interest in the original treatment.

USA Network called Jeff Lewis to say that the subject matter was "too close to home ... (and) the local cable affiliates would object." HBO Pictures (through a different contact than the one from years before) said that "on a conceptual level, this script is certainly intriguing, but we felt that Mr. Catherman's execution of his premise was problematic from both structural and characterization standpoints." (Ouch! Maybe I needed more lessons from Seger.) Atlanta producer Bill VanDerKloot, director of *Dead Aim*, the first film producer/director I was to meet, passed. So did Hemdale, again.

Networking through my job at Turner, I found the correct contact at TNT in Los Angeles, and had Jeff Lewis send a bid solicitation. Even full-time employees of Turner Broadcasting had to submit material through an agent for legal reasons. TNT was on the record in newspapers as saying that they were acquiring properties which were "on the edge," "embrace controversy," and which "take risk to test the cable movie genre."

TNT responded to the January deadline two months later, in March, with a note stating that "(U)nfortunately, this project does not fit with our programming needs at this time." Perhaps *CATV* was over the edge for them.

Chapter 4

Write!

I had learned a few things about writing, selling scripts, and myself during that first effort. I had learned to make the most of the time I had to write, whether 10 minutes or 10 hours. I needed a real agent, whether he could speak fluent German while making bone crushing tackles or not. And while I had made a career of marketing, the thing that I enjoyed about screenwriting was writing, not selling. I had to write. I had to tell a story.

In a certain interview which runs every now and then on TV, acclaimed actor Rod Steiger says the artists are the ones who produce their work not because it's necessarily fun, or to get rich, or to get famous, but because "they have to create in order to feel whole." The passion which burns deep, says Steiger, forces the urge to create.

I could relate to that. Selling a script or not, I had to write. Not doing so was no longer an option. It was time to simply write. A lot. Often. Sure, I wanted to make money at it. A lot of money would enable me to write more.

I purchased more 3" x 5" index cards and carried a bunch with me at all times. Between April, 1992 and December, 1993, I wrote six more full-length screenplays. Not surprisingly, I also enjoyed some of my most productive time at work, in the gym, and in my marriage, since passion in one area of life tends to fuel it in others.

Favorites which sparked my imagination while I was growing up were comic books, fiction like the *Tom Swift* series, and TV shows like *Captain Kangaroo, The Lone Ranger, Lassie, Superman, Roy Rogers, Sky King, The Wild Wild West, Combat,* and *Jonny Quest,* combined with more cartoons than I can remember. I loved stories and storytelling, and my mom read me a trunk load of *Golden Books.* The first book I remember was *The Runaway Pancake* (a story of daring mayhem with an escaped pancake that lives a short but exciting existence before being tricked into getting eaten). My mom and grandmother read that to me no less than 1000 times before age 5.

Three-acts-with-two-plot-points and a protagonist moving against impossible odds was a storytelling paradigm burned in long before I read Syd Field. I knew the playing field.

Because there was a nine-year difference in age between my younger brother and myself, I grew up with plenty of friends but as an "only child." As such, my mom always encouraged me to roam the woods and fields of my youth, or to take off into unknown lands on my bike, and use my imagination. Accompanied by my dog, Ginger, we could be pirates, army men, pilots, cowboys, and lion tamers all before lunch. My favorite pursuit was acting out the stories which I had read about or had seen on TV.

It was not so different writing with that imagination as an adult. Later, after trading in my typewriter for a computer, I didn't have to worry about making typographical error corrections with correcting fluid, thus saving a lot of time. The way stories came to me, I could see them in my head and hear the dialogue of the characters. I found myself having to type as fast as I could (with only two fingers) to keep up while the story unfolded in my mind's eye.

✳✳✳

I finished writing my second script, *Wings on High*, in the spring of 1992. Its premise was that an aging athlete gets a second chance in life to find peace within himself through the help of an angel. The athletic action of football and competitive bicycling formed the backdrop to the story and were autobiographical.

I had had a brief professional football tryout during college, and had recently competed in the 1990 National Bicycling championships 1-kilometer velodrome (banked track) time trial event, finishing *last* in my 35-39 year old age group. My clocking was slowed by heart medication that I was required to take during athletic competition, otherwise I would have finished second to last, I'm sure. My new Schwinn velo bike cost $289.99, and was not the high-caliber, high-tech bike that the other competitors used; one of my competitors spent over $50,000 for his wind tunnel-tested custom-made bike; if I had had a better bike, I might have finished third from last. (OK, maybe I would have finished last no matter what.)

Although I had suffered a leg injury during my earlier football training years, bicycling did not stretch and extend my hamstring leg muscle in the same way, thus allowing pain-free circular movement. I had thirsted for athletic competition for years—any competition—and in my mid-thirties had found sprint cycling on the velodrome to be the speed-addicting outlet that I craved. More important, my emphasis was on having fun, and not collecting trophies, records, or money. For a brief time, I was able to compete again, and it was a wonderful opportunity that I enjoyed for its own sake.

Most writers, I am told, write autobiographically during their first attempts, and I was no exception. The angel craze had hit America and I was no different there, either … my guardian angel and I were close friends!

＊＊＊

Two other close friends were largely the inspiration for my next script, *Wheels*, which I finished by the end of 1992. Lynn Poole, wheelchair-bound due to a spinal condition, was an expert on wheelchair aerobics who also gave motivational talks. In 1993, she won the International Association of Fitness Professionals' Christine MacIntyre Memorial Award, which carries with it a monetary donation that she pledged to the world famous Shepherd Spinal Center in Atlanta.

Bill Furbish was a boyhood friend who had been paralyzed in an accident. He went on to become a multiple medalist at the Seoul Paralympic Games. The last time I saw him perform as an athlete, I witnessed that same wonderful daredevilish look in his eye that I had seen whenever we played basketball in my driveway: Bill was playing wheelchair rugby and was in the process of ramming another guy through the gym wall. Today, he is a dad himself.

One day as I drove to work, I was thinking about the way these two lived joyful lives in the face of adversity and thinking also about the entire social movement of wheelchair access and disabilities awareness made possible through the passage of the 1990 Americans with Disabilities Act—when I accidentally pulled into a parking space reserved for the disabled. The entire story then flashed before me.

Wheels was to become a romantic comedy about an able-bodied, selfish businessman ("Ted") who is sentenced to live for one year in a wheelchair for violating his city's handicapped parking ordinance! The main character's ankle is connected to the arm of the chair by a wire. During that year, he learns about love and life from his parole officer, a beautiful woman ("Missy") who is in a wheelchair because of an injury incurred in the line of duty.

✳✳✳

I love my brother Gary. As I look back upon our relationship and how it evolved, it seems funny to me. Because of the nine-year difference in our ages, our references in life to things like history, music, film and women were separated by a huge time shift. Suddenly, however, there he was—a 22 year-old adult with an MBA, buying grown-up clothes and living in an apartment.

Having transferred out of, then back to, Atlanta, where he now was, we began meeting first by chance, then by habit, at Mom's house for Saturday brunch.

He cooked omelets, pancakes, hash browns, bacon, and biscuits while I usually jotted script notes on 3"x 5" cards. We talked about life, business, sports, women, hobbies—writing—mine, and boats—his. Sometimes we would venture out to go boat shopping, go-kart racing, golf driving range hitting, and sometimes we would simply just read and eat some more.

Brothers' Brunch, the screenplay written in the spring of 1993, was based on my relationship with Gary. The script story follows two brothers, closer in age, through forty years of life.

***

While at Turner Broadcasting in the fall of 1993, I had a marketing manager reporting to me named Sherron Martin. She had a habit of humming and singing show tunes in the office hallways and acoustically perfect restroom, and actually spent time behind the mic at jazz clubs around town. She became the inspiration for my next script, *Cleaning Up*, a musical comedy about a young white novice entertainment attorney who "discovers" his black maid as a talented singer, and the special relationship which ensues between them.

Naturally, I sent this script to singers who couldn't act, actresses who could sing, actresses who couldn't sing, agents who could or couldn't sing, Oprah Winfrey, singers who couldn't sing, Whoopi Goldberg, actresses who couldn't act, and my friends in the mail room at Creative Artists Agency. No takers. Rejections all around.

***

I love period pieces, movies that explore many different times in history. Subjects such as Christopher Columbus, pirates, old-time cowboys and all the rest allow the viewer to mentally escape, more than do movies set in the present.

While waiting in line at a grocery store check-out aisle, I picked up a copy of the March, 1993 *Disney Adventures Magazine*, the one with the tag line on the front cover "The Magazine for Kids." Perfect advertising for me. Anyway, I was flipping through it and came to an article about the history of Vikings; on one of its pages was a painting of a Viking which made me go cold, literally. I mean, I was scared to death by this wide-eyed, helmeted, cragged-toothed, bearded force of evil destruction looking at me. Nightmares ensued for two days. I knew the subject would make a great movie!

I read as many books on the subject as I could get my hands on. Truth was better than all of the myths. The Vikings contributed much to art and organized politics, let alone boat building and weaponry. But, terror was their special export.

Ruthless Viking society as we envision it came to an end because of the spread of the effect of commercial trading and the coming of Christianity. Not only was it wrong to pillage and kill, but there was much less incentive for anti-social behavior if someone was kindly shipping over some gold and clothes in return for fish and reindeer meat. You get the idea.

My script was entitled *North Wind*. A kind of *Last of the Mohicans* meets the Vikings. My story was about a Viking chieftain who sets sail for the British Isles on a typical mission to steal gold from monasteries. The monks against Vikings?! No contest. Vikings regularly invaded churches and stole valuables just as they kidnaped monks and ransomed them back to the church, or simply took them back home as slaves.

My story was about this Viking chieftain who captures a monk, avenges the murder of his Viking parents by an evil warlord, and later converts to Christianity and is baptized at the hands of his enslaved monk. The action and descriptions were as accurate as I could make them from the historical texts I read, but for the sake of storytelling, history was compressed from a few decades into a few years of time.

This script was finished by Halloween of 1993. My Viking nightmares ended by Thanksgiving.

***

At one time, I owned a house in a small town just north of Atlanta called Roswell. It was a strategic location during the Civil War (or the "War of Northern Aggression," or "The Late Unpleasantness," as it is known in the South) because its cotton and woolen mills supplied uniforms, rope, blankets, etc., to the Rebels. One old stone mill edifice today houses a small shopping mall. Public tours of the town include many antebellum homes and the beautiful old churches that were used as Yankee headquarters and hospitals. Being born in Pennsylvania, but raised in Georgia, I had rooting interests for both sides.

In fact, the 400 women and children who worked in the mill, while the boys were trying to defend Atlanta and the remains of the South, were taken captive and shipped north to Ohio, Kentucky, and places west. There, they were let go to fend for themselves, penniless and homeless, or held in work camps, or imprisoned, or "sold" as temporary employees.

My script, *Scattered Seeds*, told this story through the eyes of a young married couple—he in service to the Confederate Army, she a worker in the mill at the time of capture who gets shipped north. He and his troops are pushed 60 miles across Georgia as Sherman marched to the sea. The husband and wife each think that the other is dead. The script has a surprise ending.

In promoting the screenplay, I likened the story to a Civil War version of *Schindler's List* because the Southern captives, like their Jewish counterparts, were at times "saved" through the kindness of others during their ordeal.

The main historical text I studied was written by a Roswell policeman, Michael D. Hitt. He was a "re-enactor," meaning that every now and then he dressed up in Civil War gear and reenacted Civil War fight scenes with townsmen as fellow soldiers. His middle initial "D" stood for Douglas—Michael Douglas (!)—which I took as a good omen for this script's march to the silver screen.

Chapter 5

Glass Houses

William Goldman, the Dean of All Screenwriters of the Modern Age (*Great Waldo Pepper*, *Butch Cassidy and the Sundance Kid*, *All the President's Men*, *Maverick*) said about Hollywood, "No one knows anything." He was remarking on the fact that no one can predict which script will succeed at the box office, which actor will become a star, etc.

Therefore, in a kind of desperate screenwriter logic based on Goldman's quote, to me it seemed that every script I wrote *could* be a big success. Or something like that. You just had to believe, put your head down, and plow ahead.

I was at Turner Broadcasting in 1993, developing sales promotions for TBS, TNT, CNN, the Braves, and Hanna Barbera cartoons. Ah, how good it felt to create national promotions with Lisa DiMarzio at Paramount Pictures Marketing for movies like *Patriot Games*, *1492*: *Conquest of Paradise*, and *The Firm*, and to read Real Paramount Studio Faxes received on Real Paramount Studio Letterhead!

I had a Hollywood Hills sign—the one that spells H-O-L-L-Y-W-O-O-D—on a framed postcard hung beside the light switch of my office door. The screen saver on my computer was a downtown cityscape—LA, I imagined—encompassed by nighttime with the buildings alive with lamp lights through their glass windows—lights by which Hollywood agents were reading and discussing my screenplays, I imagined.

In late 1992 and early 1993, I was the target of a well-executed job networking campaign by Wendy Eley, the Executive Vice President Assistant for Movies & Mini Series for TriStar Television. She wanted to get back home to Atlanta from California, where she had attended Berkeley, to family and a boyfriend. Her passion was to one day become a movie or television producer. (The fact that she found a job in my department at Turner in Atlanta was a pure coincidence. Her Hollywood contacts coupled with my interest in screenwriting had nothing to do with it. Trust me.)

Wendy helped me shop my scripts to TriStar, CBS, Paramount, and others. Pass. Pass. Pass. Pass. Pass. And, pass.

My first attempts to market *Brothers' Brunch* had met a similar fate, but the rejection was more exciting. I tried to play on the "brothers" angle, and sent the script to agents for the Quaid brothers, the Baldwin brothers, the Bridges brothers, and the Sheen/Estevez duo. I figured that sending a script to brothers about playing brothers would give me an edge.

I received a call from Charlie Sheen's agent, Bill Block from International Creative Management (a major agency) in July of 1993. He passed, but for a minute, the high of being in the game was worth all the frustration. Now I was hooked for good.

It was during one of my all-consuming daydreams about Hollywood that I read a newspaper article about Sandra Glass, an Atlanta-based agent who represented professional wrestlers and rock bands (with the wrestlers as the musicians). She worked out at a gym with her clients, and entertained them in her 30,000 square foot French chateau in suburban Atlanta, on a hill overlooking the winding Chattahoochee River.

Sandra Glass and her partner Kathleen Kiley wanted to represent me. Kiley had just relocated from LA (cool!) and while she

mainly represented kids' book authors, she had "some key contacts" in the film business. After a brief introductory lunch with
Kiley, the conference call I had with Glass and Kiley went like
this:

> THEM: We want to add you to our client roster.
> ME: Great! Do we sign something?
> THEM: Yes, we (them) each receive 15% for a total of 30%
>   of each sale.
> ME: Sold!
> THEM: Don't you want to know why it's more than 10%?
> ME: OK.
> THEM: Because we're good, and because we have
>   Hollywood contacts!
> ME: OK!
> THEM: And, we won't charge incidental expenses that
>   some agents charge!
> ME: Great!
> THEM: And, we have a topnotch Hollywood attorney on
>   retainer!
> ME: Wow!
> THEM: Fox is already looking at a wrestling movie project
>   of ours.
> ME: Double wow!

So, during the spring of 1993, we agreed on a three-year contract, although the final agreement wasn't prepared until September 28. They wanted to push *Wheels*, the romantic comedy script,
and *North Wind*, my Viking script. Their attorney, Robert (Bob)
A. Finkelstein, represented, among others, George Hamilton.

George Hamilton as a Viking? I hoped not.

Max Cleland was Secretary of State for Georgia in the summer of 1993. He would one day become a U.S. Senator. His biography, *Strong at the Broken Places*, chronicled his Vietnam experi-

ence and the injury which left him a triple amputee. But, with a powerful handshake, a great mind, and a personality which flowed from strong, sincere eyes, his public life included becoming head of the U.S. Veterans Administration by appointment from (fellow Georgian) President Jimmy Carter. Max was a close friend of Sandra Glass.

Glass shared *Wheels* with him, as much to get a read on the way I had dealt with the subject of the disabled as to get an endorsement. He wrote back after reading the script:

"I am delighted you shared the screenplay, *Wheels*, with me. It encompasses a hopeful and insightful approach to humanity because Ted was able to look beyond himself and observe others from another perspective. How comforting it would be if the world could provide everyone with the opportunity to step beyond oneself and view people in an altruistic light.

"The wise and loving Missy reminds us of the enthusiasm and spiritedness that exists in all of us, and how we must return to the essential virtues of life. In a world that has proven tragedy, this story suggests that there are happy endings if you believe in the philosophy that 'life is what you make of it.'" Then Max hand wrote a P.S. which read "Great!"

This letter was circulated to all the contacts Glass was soliciting at the time. It was a major step to provide evidence that the script was not exploitative—so said one of the most politically important and courageous people in the country.

In September, I met with Max at his office at the Georgia State Capitol. He had graciously granted me some time to do a little networking. From his oversize Rolodex, I was sure he could get to Kim Basinger or Julia Roberts, two Georgia natives. Either would be perfect for the part of Missy, the wheelchair-bound love interest in *Wheels*, beautiful but tough, emotionally and physically.

Max gave me the name of Mick Basinger, Kim's brother, who lived in Jacksonville, Florida. After I explained the reason for my call, he gave me the name of her agent, Guy McElwaine at International Creative Management.

Through a huge coincidence, Kim had approached my then-second-wife, Darrah, at a bookstore in Atlanta to inquire about a place to exercise. Kim's assistant had made a note of Darrah's suggestion, and then she and her boss were quickly gone. On a long shot, I spent the remainder of the week trying to reach Kim by sending scripts addressed to her at hotels all over town. Did she receive a copy of the script? I'll never know, but if she did, she never replied. But, it was worth the chance.

My letter to Ms. Basinger's agent included what I thought was a unique proposition: if she would commit to doing the film, and then an auction held in which Hollywood producers could bid on the "package," I would guarantee that a portion of the sale price would go to a charity such as the 1996 Paralympic Games or the Shepherd Spinal Center. I interpreted the lack of response as a "pass."

Sandra Glass and Kathleen Kiley were busy promoting their wrestlers' would-be music and acting careers. To continue my marketing effort, I placed an ad in the classified section of *Variety*, which ran on October 4, 1993, and contained one sentence synopses each of *Wheels, North Wind, CATV, Brothers' Brunch*, and *Wings on High*. My ad ran alongside a list of "film projects under production," *The Paper, Speed* and others. It was a long way from one side of that page to the other, and for that matter, who could predict which films in production would be box office blockbusters and which would simply be bust?

Barry Mendel, a powerful agent from powerful United Talent, called after reading my *Variety* ad:

BARRY: I saw your ad. I want to read *North Wind*.
ME: OK.
BARRY: Do you know what I do?

ME: Sure, I read about United Talent Agency all of the time in *Variety*.

(Did I really sound like a novice, as I thought I did?)

BARRY: Be honest with me … Is this a great script?

ME: Well, people tell me that *Wheels* is my best one, but …

BARRY: I want to know whether *North Wind* is great, because if it isn't, I want you to be honest with me.
(Panic-stricken. If I answer 'yes,' and he doesn't think so, my word is no good with him, but if I answer 'no,' then why would he want to read it, or deal with a writer who doesn't believe in his own work?)

ME: Barry, this is a great script! It's action, adventure, but with a message of courage of one's convictions and …

BARRY: Send it to me.

ME: Oh, one more thing. I have an agency here in Atlanta which …

BARRY: I don't care. I get 10% of the sale. Whatever else is your business.

ME: I'll send it today!

Barry was the first of three calls that I received from the ad. The second, from Florida, asked if *North Wind* would still work if most of the cast could be naked for most of the movie. I said no. The caller hung up. The third call, from New York, was from another writer asking about the response rate to my ad, because he was thinking about doing the same. I told him to go for it, figuring that if he made it big, I'd have a friend in the industry, and if he didn't, well, it was his $300.

***

Darrah and I had been married in her hometown of Charleston, South Carolina in 1989. We returned there frequently. It is a beautiful city, full of charm, great food, history, more great food, and the arts. "Paris of the New World" was a description I have

read. We regularly attended the annual world famous Spoleto Festival, especially the chamber music since the concerts were given
at the old Dock Street Theatre, on the stage where Darrah had
starred in performances as a child. It was nearing our anniversary
in 1993 when I spotted an ad in *Variety* for a screenwriting and
film competition to be held in Charleston as part of WorldFest
Charleston. A major film festival. It felt lucky.

I got hold of an entry blank, and learned that the screenwriting
competition covered seven categories: Comedy, Dramatic-Adap-
tation, Dramatic-Original, Historical-Period Piece, Fantasy/Sci-
ence Fiction, Horror/Thriller, and Biographical. The deadline for
entries was Friday, October 1, 1993.

I entered *North Wind* in the Historical category, *Wheels* in
Comedy, and *Wings on High* in Fantasy. For $180, I was in the
game. This was the first time in 27 years that WorldFest was held
in Charleston. As well as a screenwriting competition, there were
competitions for feature films and short subject. The Festival bro-
chure noted that Steven Spielberg, George Lucas, Martin Brest,
and David Lynch each won his first significant award at this festival. The 1993 festival, in addition to seminars, had screenings of
the 50th anniversary restored versions of *Casablanca* and *Citizen
Kane*.

The envelope, please. I received a letter dated October 28,
1993, which decreed that *Wheels* had won the "Finalist Award"
(4th Place) in the comedy category! A framed certificate followed
a few weeks later.

This gave the stamp of legitimacy and objective recognition I
needed to help market all my scripts—not just *Wheels*. Oh, all
writers and performers think they themselves are good (witness
American Idol and similar competitions), and I was no exception.
Nevertheless, the award came as a total surprise, I admit, and in
an industry with such a history and standards (even Ed Wood had
style), this was a boost I welcomed.

The only unsolicited inquiry I received from winning the award came two *years* later, from a small production company based in New York that hoped to find new scripts by reading winning entries from past film festivals. They passed on *Wheels*.

In November of 1993, Sandra Glass invited Darrah and me to dinner to meet Jason Hervey, who had flown in from LA. Sandra's mansion was now almost complete, and its 30,000 square feet of space included the finest marble floors, a racquetball court, an elevator, an exercise room, a pool, and such "old world" touches as Corinthian columns, three-panel French doors with brass trim, tapestries, and a dining room seating 22 persons. The Glass fortune had been made in furniture. A lot of furniture.

Hervey, the older brother character on the TV show *The Wonder Years*, was then positioning himself as a future director/producer. A 1998 entry on the Nick At Nite *TV Land* web site listed his acting credits as beginning at age four, when he did the first of a string of 250 commercials, with one for Levi's jeans winning a Clio Award. His film credits include *The Monster Squad, Fast Times at Ridgemont High, Back to the Future*, and *Pee Wee's Big Adventure*, while his TV guest appearances range from *Alice, Baywatch Nights*, and *The Love Boat* to *Punky Brewster*, and *Taxi*. While relatively short in stature, he also excelled in some National Hockey League Celebrity All-Star Games.

Hervey loved *Wheels* and saw the script's potential, especially in light of its current social significance. However, through an interesting miscommunication, Hervey came to the meeting expecting to be hired as a producer by a "rich lady who wanted to buy her way into the business," as he said. The truth of course was that Sandra Glass was an agent trying to sell a script to a would-be producer.

Ever see two sales people try to simultaneously sell one another? It ain't pretty. Because of the misunderstanding of who was trying to do what to whom, Jason Hervey and Sandra Glass spent the meeting time, and the dinner which followed, trying to sell the other on the idea of producing *Wheels*.

It was an unproductive evening, but I liked Jason instantly. He had not only read *Wheels*, he had studied it. He had broken down all the elements—plot, subplots, characters, the action, the dialogue … everything. He had great suggestions about moving forward and seemed anxious to start. I was sure that a sale of my award-winning screenplay would soon result. It did not.

Glass was continuing to represent professional wrestlers, and thus had dealings with Scott Sassa, President of the Turner Entertainment empire, and its World Championship Wrestling cablecasts. I proposed that we invite Sassa to her mansion one afternoon, then have her client-wrestlers, dressed as Vikings, row up the Chattahoochee River in a Viking boat, "attack" the mansion, and finally act out a few key scenes from *North Wind*. I suggested that my former agent, Jeff Lewis, a real actor after all, play the lead Viking and begin the assault by shouting in German. Sassa, a Japanese-American, probably wouldn't understand German, I reasoned, but it would sound great. (And Jeff might eventually land a role in the film, thus paying him back for the free legal advice he gave me.)

Glass thought this idea was a little weird, and declined.

Sandra Glass and Kathleen Kiley let me out of my contract in March of 1994 only a few months into our "3-year deal." They said they wanted to concentrate on writing and producing, not agenting. That month I also received a rejection letter from Barry Mendel of United Talent, passing on *North Wind*. Mendel's letter read in part, the "premise was interesting, but not strong enough to pursue representation …"

We should have had the Viking wrestlers attack Sassa at the mansion.

Chapter 6

A Ride down the Path

Jason Hervey called me back in May of 1994, six months after our dinner at Sandra's house. During that time, he had formed a partnership between his company, Down the Path Productions, and another production company called Trident Entertainment, headed by David Salzberg. Neither company had produced a feature film, but Trident had done documentaries and sports videos. Hervey and Salzberg wanted to know if I had dissolved my relationship with Glass, which I said I had. Hearing that, they continued the conversation:

JASON: We want to buy an option on *Wheels*.
ME: Sold!
JASON: Do you know what an option is?
ME: No.
JASON: We have the exclusive rights for six months to
    produce your script. I'll send you a contract. And there's
    an initial payment.
ME: How much?
JASON: One dollar. For legal reasons, it has to be some
    amount.
ME: OK. Can you sign the dollar bill so I have a souvenir?
JASON: Yeah, sure …

I received the option agreement, but my dollar bill must have gotten lost in the mail. The agreement stipulated that if Hervey found studio money to produce the script, I would receive two and a half percent of the budget cost of the production of the picture, inclusive of overhead, deferred fees, and all other direct or indirect costs, but not less than $50,000. Plus, I would receive another three and three-quarters percent of the net profit earned by the movie. Other clauses spelled out earnings from sequels. Hervey could renew the option for a year for an additional dollar.

Wheels, my award-winning script, was off the market. If the production cost reached $10 million, my two and a half percent would be worth $250,000.

But in the spring of 1994, I had other things to worry about. Downsizing. Reductions-in-force. Dilbert. I was right in the mix. My department at Turner Broadcasting was relocated to New York, and I declined to relocate, thus earning a severance payment. This was the third time, but not the last, that I was to be "right-sized in a consolidating move motivated by fiscal responsibility to the share-holders in a highly competitive marketplace, blah, blah, blah." I got the ax.

Three times I had been to the unemployment line. It was as I imagined Heaven to be. All kinds of people from all walks of life, rich and poor, black and white, single and married, vested and unvested, all in the same line answering the same set of questions. The first time, my company had been purchased by a company which already had my marketing function in place. The next time, same thing. The third time, a department move to another city which I loved to visit but wouldn't want to live in.

The first time it happened, in 1986, I was working in Chicago and had been out of college for seven years. I had transferred to Chicago from Atlanta (where I had been an account executive with HBO), and had been living in Chicago less than a year. Losing my job, I felt betrayed and jaded. My first marriage was in poor shape, too, and would later end in divorce. So, there was only one thing to do in a case like this: go back to graduate school! It was the 80s thing to do, after all.

But which one? And in what field? Given my experiences and training up to that point, my cable television marketing career had topped out. I could use an MBA to restart my career, I thought.

My original academic and career plan was in the field of psychology, a subject with which I fell in love during a course in high school. I achieved only a 3.1 grade point average while attaining my Bachelor of Science in Psychology from Emory University, and given the expense of graduate school, coupled with my parents' financial problems at the time, even if I had been accepted for an advanced degree program, it would have been beyond my reach. My original career goal had been in human resource development, either on the corporate side or in a consulting capacity. Armed with the business experience I had already, should I try to recharge my interest in psychology, which I had enjoyed so much?

But what about film school?

Several film school brochures were lined up on my Chicago kitchen table, next to the MBA brochures. I studied them for days. And more days.

Or, should I just go to LA, sell cable TV door-to-door at night, write during the day, and network in the film community?

Many different factors influenced my decision and, as with most life decisions, necessary compromises had to be made. After winning a Graduate Assistantship scholarship, I decided to get a Masters degree in Sports Administration at St. Thomas University in Miami. Essentially, this was an MBA core program with such electives as sports law, human resource management, fund raising, negotiation strategy, special event marketing, and sales promotion, among many others. I felt, rightly it turned out, that with my business background, I would be able to get more from this program than if I had simply gone to graduate school right out of college. At the end, when I completed the degree, I had achieved a 3.95 grade point average from this program, considered in the field to be in the "Ivy League" of sports and event marketing. Plus, I was entering a booming field in which it would be fun to be a part. As an added bonus while at St. Thomas, I was awarded a free cruise to the Bahamas when I won a competition for writing the best 5-year marketing plan for the University's Athletic Department. I got seasick on the cruise.

This Masters degree earned in 1988, some nine years after graduating from college, jump-started my marketing career and paved the way toward future jobs on the corporate side and the agency side, dealing with professional teams, leagues, college conferences, and athletic associations. Much of my training also translated to future entertainment marketing, in which I was to engage often. However, the demands of school work, a graduate assistantship, and efforts to hold a failing marriage together didn't allow any time for writing screenplays. All I did in the way of pursuing my screenwriting career was to submit *CATV* (the first draft) to the Sundance screenwriting competition. No dice. But I always had my mind on the movie game.

If I had it to do over again, would I go to film school? Probably. But, then I might still be selling cable TV door-to-door, and could have completely missed a productive marketing career. Or, I could have sold half a dozen scripts by now. Who knows?

During my job hunt after receiving the severance check from Turner Broadcasting, Dave Salzberg called with an update to say that while he and Hervey were still trying to find a studio for *Wheels*, he had another project that he wanted to show me. So, in July of 1994, he sent me a treatment of a script entitled *Vengeance*, written by John Brascia, Robert Vincent O'Neil, and Joe Gonzalez, and acquired by Dave and Jason as a starring vehicle for Randy Travis.

Salzberg said that "one or two" studios were bidding on the project and that the movie would "definitely be made." The story concerned a modern-day cowboy who avenges the death of his brother at the hands of some drug kingpins. Randy Travis had been taking martial arts lessons to play the leading role, and the producers' goal was to begin filming by October of 1994 for a spring 1995 release date, which would coincide with a Randy Travis concert tour. Isabella Glasser (*Forever Young*) was to play the love interest, and Peter Weller (*Robocop*) was also reportedly involved.

Salzberg and Hervey liked my writing style so much, they wanted me to rewrite *Vengeance*. I would be able to put "Screenwriter" on the "Occupation" line of my 1994 tax return!

The one-page contract I received that August called for me to earn $10,538.00 for the rewrite, and to be given shared screen credit, *if* the film was made. This odd amount was a computation based on the Writers Guild minimum of $9580 for a "polish," plus 10%. A "rewrite" plus 10%, however, would have entitled me to $21,077.10, and although the technical difference between a rewrite and a polish is very subjective, I didn't quibble. Even though I was out of work at the time, I would have rewritten the entire script (which is just about what I did) for $10.53 to obtain a screen credit.

I wasn't a member of the Writers Guild, nor could I have been. In a quirky catch-22, one has to sell something first to become a member, but then one must join the Writers Guild to get further work. But in any case, Guild rates guided Salzberg's thinking.

"Sold!" said I.

In July and August, I was living the life of a full-time screenwriter, working on rewrites for *Vengeance* while making some minor changes for Hervey on *Wheels*. One change I made for Hervey's draft—and that of his fiancé—was in the name of the love-interest policewoman, "Missy," which happened to be the name of Jason's former girlfriend. So, Hervey was able to market a script with "Kelley," the name of his fiancé, and not "Missy," the cop's name.

I had found a cheap wristwatch with two faces—one for east coast and the other for west coast time—and now I really needed it!

Here was my activity schedule (east coast time) during the summer of 1994:

7:30 a	Breakfast by the pool, reading script notes
8:00	Rewrites on *Vengeance*
9:00	Let the subcontractors into our house
10:00	FAX rewrites to Salzburg and/or Hervey
11:00	Follow-up on personal job leads
1:00 p	Go to mailbox to look for unemployment check, and mail resumes
2:00	Receive FAX notes from Salzburg and/or Hervey
3:00	More rewrites
4:00	Give subcontractors a portion of the life savings I was sinking into the 56-year old, $500,000 money pit house
5:00	Lift weights, run, swim, smoke cigar
7:00	Dinner with Darrah; discussion of selling the house before the baby comes (yes, she was also pregnant with our first child, Andy)
10:00	More rewrites (while watching *The Money Pit* for a morale boost)
11:00	Asleep, dreaming of being a screenwriter able to afford my lifestyle and a new roof.

By the end of summer, I had more than enough material to write my own version of *The Money Pit* and to play the Tom Hanks' role. *Vengeance*, the script which would "definitely be made," was completed, and never filmed. We eventually sold the house.

Novelist Anne Rivers Siddons lived in a house across from ours, so I wasn't even the best writer on the street!

On my 39th birthday, November 28, I wrote a letter of reply to Sandra Glass who had telephoned to say she had formed a film production company, had "some Hollywood financial backing," and would give "strong consideration" to producing *Wheels* as her first project. I explained to her that Hervey had an option on it, but that my other six screenplays were available. Pass. She didn't want to deal with Hervey in a joint production, and she wasn't interested in any of my scripts other than *Wheels*. (She could have filmed most of my Viking script *North Wind* in the woods surrounding her mansion, and saved a lot of money.)

At some point, Hervey communicated that he was still continuing to pursue *Wheels*, and that his agent at powerhouse Creative Artists Agency was trying to pitch it to Steve Martin to play the lead, and secondly to Ministry Pictures (through a production deal with Columbia). He had high hopes.

Alas, Hervey's option lapsed without a sale and without renewal in 1995. Would I ever sell a screenplay?

Chapter 7

It's a Wonderful Life

May 22, 1976. Texas Stadium, Dallas. Home of the World Champion Dallas Cowboys. I was there along with a few hundred other wannabes, trying out for the Dallas Cowboys. The most important test of the day came with the running of the forty-yard dash. An article in the August 10, 1998, issue of *Sports Illustrated* attributed this somewhat arbitrary forty yard distance to the legendary NFL Coach Paul Brown, who assumed in the 1960s that that was as far as a football player would run on an average play. Most NFL teams had used the 100 or 50 yard standard in the 1950s. Obviously, times are faster on artificial turf than on grass, and NFL scouts do their own timing rather than rely on other reports.

It is amazing how much difference a tenth of second can mean to a coach (and the player's agent, if he has one). How much? Millions of dollars. The forty, reliable or not, is a key indicator of future employment in the NFL, at least to the scouts.

That day in Dallas, I didn't have an agent. I didn't even have a college team. Twice in high school, I was taken out of sports because of heart trouble diagnosed as Wolf-Parkinson-White syndrome. While in college at Emory University, a new family of medications was tested on me, and I was allowed to participate in sports again. My dream in high school, where I was a running back, had been to attend Georgia Tech and play football. I would have played wide-receiver in college. My real love was returning punts and kicks.

So I hadn't played football since my junior year of high school, and hadn't participated in any organized sports since the spring of that year when, having had uncontrollable heart palpitations during a track practice, had to quit the team. People had died sudden deaths because of this arrhythmia, and Dad and the coaching staff now decided to take the conservative medical advice. I was able to get back into high school sports while in 9th grade, after my first major heart episode had deprived me of a year away from sports, because Dad found a cardiologist who agreed to sign my medical waiver, reasoning that the palpitations had caused no lasting damage to my heart.

Today, decades later, a simple heart "ablation" procedure for pediatric patients as well as pro athletes can correct the problem, with no side effects and no hindrance to physical performance as opposed to taking medication. I had my own successful heart procedure performed in 2007 by Dr. Niraj Sharma at St. Joseph's Hospital in Atlanta.

Dallas was holding tryouts for anyone who wanted to show up. Former players from college, the pros, the brick yards, and the business offices all came. I had read that, even for the Cowboys in years past, players without any college experience were allowed to try out. I called the Cowboy office, told them I was still in college, and they said it didn't matter. I was eligible. And I was then, as I am now, always drawn to the most impossible of dreams (what other kind are there?). I borrowed a couple of hundred dollars from my boyhood friend Tommy Smith and was off (reimbursing Tommy with cheeseburgers and money from my part-time college job as the Miller Brewing Company College Marketing Representative at Emory University, organizing special beer events and local beer advertising).

For a receiver, 4.4 seconds in the forty-yard dash was considered excellent by NFL standards. That, and the ability to catch the ball. The fastest forty ever recorded was 4.16 seconds, clocked by the eventual NFL receiver Laveranues Coles, in 1998. The much heralded Deion Sanders, also from Florida State, once ran a 4.29-second forty at a scouting combine in 1989. From 1988 to 1998, only 18 players ran a sub-4.4 second forty yard dash, according to one report.

In Dallas, at the tryout that day, I clocked back-to-back 4.3 second forty-yard sprints. Dallas Coaches surrounded me, grabbing my sign-up sheet from a stack. I knew something was up.

Condensed version of the next scene:

COACH: This is the kind of speed we look for in camp. Aren't many in the NFL this fast. We can teach you to play, but we can't teach speed.

ME: Uh, thanks. Sir. Uh, Coach.

COACH: (reading, eyes going wide, a pained expression crossing his face) But, damn, you aren't *eligible* this year, or …

ME: What?! But I called your office and they said …

COACH: (calming voice) Look, you aren't going to get any faster. Or taller. So, just stay healthy. I wouldn't transfer to play anywhere if I were you. You might get hurt. Just stay healthy and come back again. The NFL has an agreement with the colleges not to take current students.

Back at the fraternity house, the guys in pre-law told me to sue the NFL for restraint of trade. This was many years before Herschel Walker threatened to sue the NFL, and Maurice Clarett finally did and failed, but the League eventually relaxed their policy and starting grabbing underclassmen. Anyway, how could I sue a potential employer? Didn't seem like a way to make friends.

What I didn't know was that on that particular day I was in the best shape I would ever be in my life. Ever. The next tryout in Dallas never happened for me because during the following year, I pulled my right hamstring muscle. The leg bothers me to this day, especially in the cold. In retrospect, I should have had surgery to repair it.

I went to over twenty different doctors, chiropractors, kinesiologists, and various other therapists. Each had a different treatment. Each laughed aloud at the methods of the others. Clyde Partin, who was a pre-med fraternity brother and future godfather to my son Andy, recommended leeches. The only truly honest opinion was given to me by Jerry Rhea, the Atlanta Falcon trainer (and once NFL Trainer of the Year): "I have no idea what to do." Neither did anyone else, although that didn't stop them from charging me.

I should have tried the leeches.

My Dad told me the same thing he had told me the previous two times I had been bumped from sports for the sake of my heart: "There's more to life than football. So much more. It's time to dream another dream." Dad's own promising athletic career had been cut short by medical problems, and he had successfully battled cancer on a few occasions. He knew about adversity and how dealing with it helps one gain perspective.

My son Andy was born on March 9, 1995. A few months later, on the day of his baptism, as Darrah held him, and his head bobbed around, pensively looking over the congregation of unfamiliar faces, his gaze suddenly locked on my own as I stood next to him. Andy smiled at me, and in his small blue eyes I saw God's reflection of pure love.

Dad was right.

***

A few Hollywood directories list producers who accept scripts without an agent's introduction. I tapped into one of these in early 1995, and sent out a mailing to 46 producers, each with a letter of introduction, a brief synopsis of each of my scripts, and the customary self-addressed stamped envelope. By year-end, 19 had responded, of whom 10 asked to read one or more scripts. Out they went, only to be returned with more nice rejections from everybody.

Next!

"How about some other approaches to try to get to people that one can't get to?" I asked myself. I sent *North Wind* to Ed Harris and Robert De Niro in care of their restaurant in New York, the Tribeca Grill. Years later, I was able to eat there, saw the door through which my envelope must have come, and actually caught a glimpse of De Niro as he left his office above the restaurant. I never received a reply from them.

Next!

Doing some LA networking by sending letters and the script of *North Wind* to history professors of the University of Southern California, I attempted to get an academic "endorsement." Who knows, I thought, they might enjoy the script, want to sign on as the film's "history consultant," and help to sell it to some movie mogul who lived next door. You have to admit, it was creative thinking. Well, at least desperate thinking, but maybe creative, too.

The return mail from the USC history department urged me to find an agent.

Next!

There was Jim "Mattress Mack" McIngvale of Houston, Texas. He sells about $70 million of discount furniture a year, and personally funded the $18 million production of *Sidekicks*, a Chuck Norris action picture. Chuck had met McIngvale's wife Linda at a Houston fundraiser. *Variety* reported that Mack was developing other projects of a more "sensitive" nature, and that spurred me to send him *Wheels*. I never received a reply, although the clerks at his store were always nice to me when I called trying to reach the Mattress King.

Next!

In late 1994, an ad appeared that called for "true story" scripts to be sent to a post office box for K.C. Productions. K.C. Productions, I was to learn, was Kris Capra's company. Kris was the wife of Tom Capra, the nephew of the legendary Frank Capra (*It's a Wonderful Life*).

Replying to my letter, Kris asked to read *CATV*, *Cleaning Up*, and *Wheels*. She was repped by Steve Weiss at William Morris, who was helping package production deals for her. At the end of a few months of letters and phone calls, for one reason or another ("wouldn't work on TV," etc.) one by one, the scripts were rejected.

Next!

More than a year after I had stood in an unemployment line due to the Turner "reorganization," I received a call from Keith Finger, whom I had met in line since we were both out-of-work marketers. Keith and I immediately hit it off, and we shared some job leads. As an afterthought, I had told him to please call me if he ever ran into anyone with Hollywood connections.

KEITH: Hey, remember me? Keith Finger. From the Department of Labor.

ME: Uh, yeah.

KEITH: You said to call with Hollywood leads.

ME: Oh, Keith! I remember! Yes, how are you?!

KEITH: Good. Anyway, I had to track you down to give you this lead.

ME: OK, shoot.

KEITH: My dentist.

ME: You're at the dentist?

KEITH: No, my dentist is the Hollywood connection!

ME: Huh?

KEITH: Yeah, really! He co-produced Sly Stallone's *Over the Top!*

ME: Huh?

KEITH: Yeah. He's connected. Here's his number …

Sure enough, Dr. Peter Mills of Atlanta was a Producer/Dentist. Specifically, he was an orthodontist who had many celebrity clients. He gave out refrigerator magnets in the shape of a big tooth inscribed with "Peter B. Mills, D.D.S., ORTHODONTIST TO THE STARS, BRACE YOURSELF FOR ANOTHER DAY."

I asked him why, after his first successful movie venture, he hadn't moved to LA and worked full-time as a producer. "I just love orthodontia," he said. You have to admire professional dedication and passion like that. He also made specialized golf putters of exotic woods, leather, and precious metals.

He had formed a loose partnership of sorts with two other Atlantans, Neal Hoyt (former Turner Broadcasting executive) and Tony Escandari (home builder). They were brainstorming and networking for possible future film and television projects. Tony had shot a 30-minute drama pilot, with a cameo appearance by heavyweight boxing champ Evander Holyfield, that he was shopping to the networks while building Holyfield's mansion in south Atlanta.

One of their ideas was to transform The Champ into a superhero movie character (a la Stallone or Schwarzenegger) after his boxing days were over. On spec, I wrote a few movie outlines that capitalized on Holyfield's athletic talents. The partners liked them, as they did my other scripts.

Through Dr. Mills, I once met The Champ. He had a smaller waist than I did, hands the size of catchers' mitts, and the smile of a man at peace with himself.

While the partners were waiting for Holyfield to retire, home builder Tony Escandari approached me about another script idea. He had a two-page outline about a psychotic doctor who had created a virus to enable his pharmaceutical company to benefit. We signed an agreement to split any profit from the movie should it ever be made, and I went to work on it in August, 1995. No up front payment to me.

I was finished with the first draft in October. *Eye of Justice* became my ninth script and boasted some of my best writing. Tony wanted to make some changes—large and small, but I declined to go along. I reasoned that whoever produced, directed, or starred in the film—all of them would want to make tons of changes. Why not deal with them all at once? And wouldn't those who would make the film have more to say than Tony? He and I agreed upon the basic story as reflected in the 2-page outline. I was committed to playing this game but I insisted on playing by my rules since there was no guarantee that the film would be made. I was working for free at that point, after all.

Meanwhile, Tony was building Evander Holyfield's $15 million house, and expanding his clientele to include other celebrities. Evander's house was larger than Sandra Glass'—the Champ's was 54,000 square feet, with 17 bathrooms, eight bedrooms, three kitchens, a bowling alley, an Olympic-sized swimming pool, two five-car garages, and a 135-seat movie theatre. Reported annual upkeep totaled $1.2 million. According to Escandari's web site for his Tuscany Builders, the house was America's twelfth largest.

Evander told a reporter that he was going to open the house for tours only to poor children, in hopes of inspiring them. "I'm not showing the house to another rich person," said the Champ.

Escandari's networking skills were excellent, and he was very charming, professional and charismatic. A Sicilian, he looked like Al Pacino.

Conversation in 1996:

TONY: We're making progress on *Eye of Justice*.

ME: Have you raised any money?

TONY: Commitments from my contacts total 50 million dollars.

ME: Huh?!

TONY: 50 million dollars.

ME: When do we start shooting?!

TONY: After we have the cast and director.

ME: Anybody in mind?

TONY: Bruce Willis for the lead.

ME: Perfect! Have you pitched his agent?

TONY: No. Don't need to.

ME: Huh?

TONY: I sat next to him at a fight. I don't want to work through agents.

ME: Huh?

TONY: Personal relationships. That's how I'm going to get the talent.

ME: OK, but did he like the script?

TONY: I didn't discuss it with him. Too early.

ME: Huh?

TONY: I need to build some relationships. It'll take some time.

ME: Huh?

TONY: When I have a good relationship with him, he'll say "yes."

ME: And the director?

TONY: Same thing.

ME: Anyone in mind?

TONY: Not yet. This might take years, but it'll be worth it.

ME: Wanna buy me out?

TONY: No.

Huh?

(Note to Bruce Willis: here's a great action script waiting for you—kind of like *Patriot Games* meets *Three Days of the Condor*.)

✳✳✳

September of 1995, and still without an agent, I replied to an ad in *Variety* which read, "New Licensed Signatory Agency looking for new material! All subjects welcomed! Contact Hopkins & Hopkins."

I sent a 20-pound box of my scripts to Charles Hopkins at his office in Frankfort, Indiana. The Hopkins of the first part was his wife, owner of some video stores.

Charles Hopkins replied that he had received hundreds of scripts, but would select a half-dozen writers to go along with the few writers and actors he already had in his stable. He liked *North Wind* and my Civil War script *Scattered Seeds*, and wanted to represent me. I signed a 17-page contract which included a lot of Writers Guild boilerplate, and a stipulation that I would pay him a standard $75 per quarter to cover miscellaneous expenses. He was to receive a standard 10% commission.

After I finished *Eye of Justice*, I sent him a copy and told him of the $50 million war chest that Tony Escandari had put together. Charles Hopkins had gotten into the business as a movie set designer, and although based in Indiana, had a network of contacts from coast to coast.

Hopkins liked *Eye of Justice*, and immediately set about putting together a package of talent to which (he believed) Tony Escandari could not say "no." Hopkins obtained commitments of sorts—that is, depending on the money—from Linda Kozlowski (*Crocodile Dundee*), international star Rutger Hauer (*Nighthawks*, *Hostile Waters*), and producer Paul Freeman (*North and South*). Holes in their respective schedules meant filming could start within months, not years. This would be my big break. I could just feel it.

Tony however, claiming he had "secured" Sidney Poitier as co-star, and still wanting Bruce Willis for the lead, passed on the Hopkins' package.

From his office in Indiana, Hopkins continued his efforts to pitch my other scripts. His contacts led him to send *Wheels* to Sean Young (*Cousins, No Way Out, Wall Street*). Young was looking for a project to produce, direct, and star in. I thought she would be great for the role of the wheelchair-bound police officer. Sadly, she passed on the script.

Other Hopkins' pitches included sending *North Wind* to Mel Gibson, action tough guy Steven Seagal, and the Jesuit-owned film company Paulist Pictures (*The Black Robe, The Mission*), the latter I had learned about from my brother's best friend, Jack Butler, who was studying to become a Jesuit priest.

Strike one. Strike two. Strike three.

Here is what I was up against: In 1996 the Writers Guild estimated that a total of about 25,000 scripts were submitted for registration. At that time about 300 films were made each year. And, according to *Script* magazine, only 457 scripts were purchased (not necessarily all written in 1996). The most popular genre was comedy (136), followed by drama (115), action/adventure (79), thrillers (68), sci fi (27), romance (9), family fare (6), horror (5), animation (4), fantasy (3), westerns (3), and musicals (2). The odds were long, and the effort to get a sale was something out of *Homer* (not Simpson).

My friends, clients and employees continued to help me, despite the odds. Employee/friend Cloud Conrad was able to get me a read with Chris Svoboda who was with Debra Hill Productions (*Halloween, Adventure in Babysitting, The Fisher King, The Mirror Has Two Faces, Escape from LA*). Svoboda requested *Wheels, Brothers' Brunch, Wings on High*, and *CATV*. Client/friend John Hurley was able to get *Wheels* and *Scattered Seeds* to producer Suzanne de Passe (*Lonesome Dove*) through his brother-in-law who was her hair dresser. The responses from these producers were the same: "These do not meet our development needs at this time."

***

Sometimes scripts take an angel to get them going. One of my favorite stories about one of my favorite movies began when a writer got an idea, while he was shaving one morning, about a man who contemplates suicide and wishes he was never born. This short story was entitled *The Greatest Gift*, and began as a pamphlet which turned into that writer's Christmas card. The movie starred a young man who was just out of the war and was about to go back to his family's hardware business because he had had no offers to act. The angel called him. The movie lost $480,000.

The angel was Frank Capra. The young actor was Jimmy Stewart. The movie was *It's a Wonderful Life*. Frank Capra once said, "You get to speak to millions of people in the dark."

It's a privilege I hoped I would also have. Would it ever come?

Chapter 8

Cause Marketing

"Rejection breeds obsession."

"Luck doesn't happen by mistake."

Those two lines belong to movie mogul Robert Evans, who used them in his book *The Kid Stays in the Picture*. But they apply to just about every artist, writer, and wannabe anything else. I was obsessed with the need for some publicity "buzz," and I needed some "heat" to make luck happen.

Suppose I looked at selling my scripts as a marketing puzzle instead of a writing puzzle. After all, my career centered on marketing everything from cable TV to cars, motor oil to movies; so maybe the pieces of the puzzle would fit together better if I regarded my scripts as "clients."

The term "cause marketing" was coined by a marketer for American Express Cards, Jerry Welsh. Unlike corporate philanthropy which is merely giving money to charitable organizations, cause marketing is more sophisticated: the company and the charity both promote the "cause," and the company rewards the charity with a portion of its sales revenue. Example: Every time you use your American Express Card, AMEX would donate a percentage of the total to the Statue of Liberty Restoration Fund, Food for the Poor, or some other worthy cause.

I heard Jerry speak at a marketing convention in 1993. His message: Develop a Big Idea. "Nobody likes little ideas."

I contacted Jerry and told him my Big Idea: create a cause marketing event in which Hollywood producers and members of the general public are invited to buy tickets to an auction in which film rights to my screenplay *Wheels* would be sold to the highest bidder. Part of the proceeds realized would go toward the 1996 Paralympic Games and other charities that help the physically-challenged, such as those devoted to spinal research. Of course, Welsh would get a "management fee." Others involved (I recommended Creative Artist Agency's then-prez Mike Ovitz) would also get a cut, proportionate to the role they played and the effort they made.

Jerry called back to say he thought this was a Big Idea, but that he was working on other Big Ideas of his own and didn't have time to work with me. However, he would share *Wheels* with his old classmate from Harvard, John Kael (*sex, lies and videotape, Mr. Baseball*). I never received a response.

I also pitched my Cause Marketing Big Idea, regarding the *Wheels* Charity Auction, to the 1996 Paralympic Games, The Miami Project's spinal research center, The American Paralysis Association (and hence Christopher Reeve), The Mike Utley Foundation, Planet Hollywood (owners Arnold Schwarzenegger, Bruce Willis, and Sly Stallone), The National Council on Spinal Cord Injury, and The Carter Center. All passed for one reason or another.

Time to buy another filing cabinet to hold all of the rejections.

While I continued to do battle for my Cause Marketing Big Idea, I was improving my skills as a face-to-face Hollywood "networker." It's a fine line between that, and being a "pest." Or worse, an overtly (obnoxious) "salesman." It takes finesse, really, to be able to move a conversation to an area where sits your own agenda, all the while persuading your captives that it was their idea.

Telemarketers who called in the evening to sell every service imaginable would immediately find themselves participating in a question and answer session of my own devising: Who do you know in Hollywood? Do you think he might want to read a screenplay of mine?

No one was safe.

My friends would watch and listen in amazement, sometimes recording my networking exploits with their watches, to see how quickly I could move a conversation which began with any topic from world famine, the stock market, or the correct situations for a suicide squeeze in the ninth inning, to whom they might know in LA or in the movie business. Sometimes people went out of their way, in the end, to help a struggling screenwriter.

I felt I wasn't using people in the sense of exploiting them for a short-term benefit in senseless, corporate, Dilbert-like infighting, but rather enlisting their involvement in something they found intriguing. Since selling a screenplay is comparable to winning the lottery (both in odds and sometimes cash), most people were gladly willing to help. They sensed my excitement and wanted to be part of something grand and adventurous. (And I promised a commission.)

The most amazing thing was how many people were connected to LA or the movie business even if they didn't realize it at first. Whether it was the guy behind the counter at the pharmacy, the computer repairman, or the intern in the mailroom, if I asked the right questions, I very often found someone who it turned out, knew *someone.*

At the height of my prowess in conversation-steering, I found myself in June of 1996 seated on an Atlanta-to-Los Angeles flight next to a beautiful, intelligent young woman. Before instructions about seat belt safety and the nearest exit row were read, we had learned that I was a businessman heading to LA for a meeting and she was a real estate agent having just come from a family reunion in Birmingham, Alabama. I wanted to be a screenwriter someday, and thus my impending meeting with Warner Brothers, even on unrelated business, was a high. She was actually an animation film screenwriter earning a living selling real estate. She, unlike me and the thousands of other wannabes, had the guts to pack up and go to LA to pursue her screen dream. All this was divulged before the plane taxied down the runway for a four-hour flight.

She didn't stand a chance. She sat next to the window and I was in the aisle seat beside her. She couldn't escape. Poor Christine Hughes. Trapped!

Christine turned out to be one of the most gracious people I have ever met. She had a rare inner joy and radiance. Fate, the work of angels—whatever you wish to call it—was there on that flight as I sat next to her. In retrospect, I couldn't possibly have sat next to anyone else on that crowded flight.

She asked for, and I quickly provided, one-page synopses for all nine of my screenplays. Since I had to retrieve my briefcase from the overhead rack while the plane was still climbing and the fasten-seat-belt light still on, I caught a disapproving glance from a flight attendant. But hey, if the plane was going down during take-off, I was going down pitching a script, and Christine might be the only survivor!

She read the pages intently and then pointed to the paragraph of *Wheels* with a knowing smile. "This one," she said. "I think I know someone who can help you."

Christine had worked as a volunteer for Dr. Ted Baehr to help coordinate his annual version of the Oscars, The Sir John Templeton Awards, giving accolades to film professionals whose movies had moral fiber, love and virtue. He has written several books including *Hollywood's Reel of Fortune* and *The Media-Wise Family*, has produced and financed TV and film projects, and is a syndicated radio commentator.

Baehr was also Chairman of the Christian Film & Television Commission and was Publisher of *Movieguide*, a film review magazine. He lived in Atlanta at that time, though he was then planning to move to LA.

I contacted Baehr when I returned to Atlanta, outlining in my letter the Cause Marketing Big Idea for an auction for *Wheels*. I proposed that he and Chris Reeve co-chair the event, and that he receive a commission for helping to publicize it. The proceeds raised would go to Manuel and Sheila Cardenas, an Atlanta couple who were a 1996 Paralympic Games merchandise licensee, and who spent their lives raising money to buy wheelchairs for two million people in Ecuador who had no mobility. I met with Sheila, a pediatrician, who showed me pictures of disabled people literally getting around in shopping carts or sitting on skateboards.

While Baehr found the concept of the black-tie-dinner fundraiser both novel and worthwhile, his schedule didn't permit him the time required to pull it off. He was in the midst of moving his magazine and his efforts to "minister to the film community" to Los Angeles. I told him that I was appreciative of his review of my idea, though, and when I asked him for guidance to find an agent, he suggested Terry Porter of Flat Rock, Indiana.

✳✳✳

Flat Rock, Indiana. Population 300, depending on who is out of town on vacation, or who may be visiting. Forty miles southeast of Indianapolis, Flat Rock is surrounded by cornfields and boasts one gas station, a Lutheran church, a white concrete-block fire station, and a lawn mower repair shop. Just outside of town stands Terry Porter's 150 year-old brick farmhouse. There, on the second floor, he ran Agape Productions and Flat Rock Records. Both an agent and producer, he represented screenwriters, TV writers and novelists, as well as music artists on his record label. Representing about 80 clients and espousing Midwestern, Christian values, Terry has sold scripts for all of the *Star Trek* spinoffs,

The X-Files, Xena: Warrior Princess, Touched by an Angel, Dr. Quinn, Medicine Woman and *Walker: Texas Ranger.* He and partner Dave Ruiz made sales trips to LA about five times a year.

Porter got his start in show business as the drummer for the Lemon Pipers, banging out their 1968 hit *Green Tambourine.* His love of music had led him to start a record label of blues, folk, and storytelling artists, and to produce movie and documentary soundtracks.

Porter loved *Wheels, North Wind,* and *Cleaning Up* and wanted to represent me. He found in these stories the kind of Christian values he looked for in scripts, while refusing numerous screenplays from other writers who gloried in gratuitous sex or violence.

Meanwhile, Charles Hopkins of Frankfort, Indiana (population 14,754), whom I never got to meet face to face, had made a valiant effort to pitch my scripts before a career choice brought him to producing low-budget films of his own. (His first project was a "true-life horror film set in a swamp in New Jersey.") When Charles let me out of my contract, I signed a one-year agreement with Porter on July 29, 1996. Same terms: 10% commission and $75 a quarter for expenses.

Neither Hopkins nor Porter knew of the other's agency, or even the whereabouts of the other's Indiana town.

It wouldn't be until October of 1997 that I would meet Terry Porter face to face, on one of his trips to Atlanta to confer with Turner Broadcasting people about producing soundtracks for documentaries. Terry is one of the most genuine, most sincere people in the world.

✳✳✳

When I ran across the publication *ABILITY* in the spring of 1997, my interest in pushing my Cause Marketing Big Idea *Wheels* Fund Raising Project came to life again. The magazine carried an article about Connie Stevens, the film icon of the 1960's, and a Board Member of the Community Entry Services (CES) Foundation in Jackson Hole, Wyoming. CES provides opportunities for work and home ownership for persons with disabilities, and runs the Connie Stevens Center, a 155-person building which houses people between the ages of 13 and 40. CES is dedicated to empowering people to maximize their independence and lead productive lives in the community. Celebrity events, some on snow and some not, fill out an aggressive fund raising calendar.

I sent a letter to Ms. Stevens pitching my Cause Marketing Big Idea *Wheels* auction (proceeds going to CES), and received a reply from Carol Bowers, the Director and Vice Chairman of CES. Her letter cited an article in *The Chronicle of Philanthropy* in which a Catholic boys home had produced a film, sold it, and "made quite a large profit." In a subsequent phone call she requested a copy of the script *Wheels*, which I sent immediately.

In my last conversation with her, she indicated she would put my proposal before the CES Board in June, 1997—to explore either the "auction" idea or the possibility of buying the script outright for their own production. After repeated attempts, I never heard from her again.

Chapter 9

So Close, So Far

Joel Schumacher is a Living Film Legend. He has directed *Batman and Robin, Batman Forever, The Client, A Time to Kill, St. Elmo's Fire, The Lost Boys, Cousins, Flatliners, Dying Young, Falling Down, The Incredible Shrinking Woman*, and others. You get the idea.

In 1997, I was working as the Senior Manager of National Promotions for the prepaid phone card division of MCI, the telecommunications company. My job was to develop promotions to help retailers sell phone cards, and to persuade product companies such as coffee manufacturers to use phone cards as gifts for consumers when selling their French Roast, for example. MCI purchased licenses from the movie studios and major sports leagues such as those in baseball so that players, actors, and logos could be pictured on phone cards and make them more attractive to customers. A phone card collectors market sprung up. After all, a phone card or any prepaid card is a handy thing to have in your pocket.

MCI was a licensee of *Batman and Robin*, and a poster of the movie hung in my office. At eye level, I could read Joel Schumacher's name in the small print. Before one meeting in Hollywood with the Warner Brothers marketers, we visited several *Batman and Robin* sets on the day after a shoot, then went into a viewing room to see the raw footage from scenes shot on the sound stage where we had just been. It was an electric feeling. Magic.

Before another meeting with the Warner Brothers marketers, we walked on a tour of the WB studio backlot. More magic. Walking along roads, onto sets, and in the sound stages where hundreds of movies and TV shows had been shot, and where hundreds of stars had stood, was surreal for me. City streets faded quickly into a suburban neighborhood, then a western town with the famous saloon that had been witness to hundreds of fist fights. Just around the corner was the jungle/swamp set where John Wayne soldiered in *The Green Berets* which my Dad and I had seen one night during a summer vacation. That same swamp (actually a cement pond) was where the Budweiser "frog" commercials were shot. Even more magic.

It was like first seeing the presents under the tree on Christmas morning, the very first Christmas I can remember—every single second of the studio tour was like that. It was also like being Dorothy, stepping outside her house into Munchkinland and realizing this wasn't Kansas (although I've never been to Kansas, and certainly mean no disrespect to Kansans anywhere).

One time a member of our group spotted Arnold The Future Governor riding in an RV across the WB lot, stogie in hand. I caught a whiff of his cigar even before I saw him. Being a cigar smoker myself, I could tell it was a good quality smoke. Another time, George Clooney was sitting at a bench, eating lunch in his *ER* scrubs. Both were members of Joel's Team Gotham.

It was particularly exciting when, on May 21, 1997, I joined a few hundred attendees of the Promotion Marketing Association of America's entertainment marketing conference to hear Joel address us at a luncheon. He spoke of the relationship between licensees and corporate marketing partners who develop plans for supporting a movie, and the value in having movie characters appear on boxes of cereal brands that Joel swore he ate.

During the weeks leading up to the conference, I had rehearsed in my mind the many scenarios under which I might come face to face with Joel Schumacher. I had also stuffed some script synopses in my briefcase, standard for any trip to LA, given the (unlikely) chance of meeting someone on the plane or at the hotel who might help me. Actually, I had found my then-current agent, Terry Porter, on just such a chance encounter on a plane trip.

After Joel's talk about the soon to be released *Batman* movie, about how he loved the cast, and about how his passion for movies burned deeply, he took questions. Several people roamed the audience with handheld microphones. With the raise of a hand, anyone could ask Joel anything. He answered questions about the actors he would like to work with that he hadn't (answer: Tom Cruise, Brad Pitt), and what he ate for breakfast (answer: the sponsor's cereal brand, of course).

My hand went up. I was handed the microphone.

It's funny what goes through your mind at times like these. Seconds become frozen into hours. I had to quickly weigh several factors: the fact that there were many other hands raised, and like having to urinate in a public bathroom with several others waiting in line behind you, I felt a sense of urgency. And slight panic. Also, in a dream I had the night before, I had bolted the doors to the ballroom, and then grabbed my butter knife from the luncheon table and held it to a woman's neck while another woman read *Wheels* aloud to Joel, who was forced to listen while he played a violin, but there were no violins in the room, and I didn't know if he could even play.

My voice cracked. I asked Joel whether he thought the movement to raise awareness of the disabled in the U.S. was a good theme that Hollywood ought to embrace, and whether if there was in fact a good script out there with this theme, he would direct it even though it wouldn't be on the same blockbuster level as, say, *Batman*. Or something like that.

Joel replied that the disabled and wheelchair accessibility were very important, and some fine movies had been made with that theme, and that, yes, with the right story, he would love to direct such a picture! In fact, he imparted, in a comic book many years ago, Bruce Wayne had broken a leg and was forced into a wheelchair himself. Several hands shot up around the room, evidently assuming that I had finished my line of questioning.

I hadn't. So, I continued ... even if the story wasn't a special effects story? ... No, said Joel, the story is what counts. He stared at me in silence as more hands were raised around me. I remember his beaming smile and his penetrating, haunting eyes.

I slowly moved the mic to my lips once again. "Thanks, Mr. Schumacher." My interview was over.

Should I have asked if he wanted to read *Wheels*? Or, somewhat more politely, asked permission for my agent to send the script to his agent (which anyone could do, anyway)? Whose etiquette was overriding here? That of a business banquet? Or a desperate writer? Or both? Are they perhaps the same?

Visions of Robert De Niro in *King of Comedy* flashed before my eyes.

In that instant of clarity, as I thanked Joel, I decided that what mattered most was not whether I was hogging the mic, or whether the banquet hosts would be embarrassed by my personal queries, although they were very important to me. No, what consumed me was that I didn't want to embarrass Joel in any way, or place him in a potentially disagreeable situation of having to say no, to a question that asked in a more appropriate situation might have elicited a yes. Who would that benefit? To ask him blatantly in a crowded room if I could send him *Wheels* would be an affront. The fact that from all accounts he's one of the nicest people on earth, and might have felt constrained to agree, would make the affront that much worse. I decided that even while being desperate, and despite my first inclination to press the situation, I was going to be professional. I might be a hack in the final analysis, but I was to go down as a professional hack. Professional courtesy was called for here.

I'll bet half of the readers would have done the same as I did. (The other half would have gone for the butter knife.)

Like Batman himself, Joel disappeared behind the curtain after the last question, and was gone. I was hoping that he would stay just a while longer and mill around with the crowd, where I would ask him, point blank, if I could pitch him an idea, or several ideas, right then and there. Whatever his answers, I could accept it. But he was gone.

Lunch was over. I sprinted to the nearest elevator and to my room and made three phone calls. I dialed The Directors' Guild and got the name and number of Joel's law firm, who referred me to his agent, Bryan Lourd, at Creative Artists Agency. I tried to call Terry Porter with the name of Joel's agent, and Joel's "interest" in directing a "good story about the disabled." It was a hot lead, as far as I was concerned, but Terry was out of the office.

The next day, May 22, the 21st anniversary of my attempt to make the Dallas Cowboys, the newspapers on the flight home to Atlanta featured pictures and descriptions of "Share a Smile Becky," Barbie's new doll pal who has strawberry blond hair, bendable joints, and sits in a pink wheelchair. Mattel's Marla Libraty said, "The doll will showcase the richness and the diversity that we see in the real world today." Twenty-one years apart to the day: two completely different events which signaled that I was so close, but yet so far, from achieving a dream.

At home, I relayed my brush with Joel Schumacher to my then-wife Darrah. Her reaction was instantaneous and without compromise: "What?! You didn't try to close him on the spot?! After all you've been through?! You didn't walk right up and shove a copy of *Wheels* in his face?!" I'll bet half of my readers would agree with Darrah. (OK, maybe more than half.) After all, I had placed a license plate on the front of her car which read "California," so she was certainly as qualified as anyone to have an opinion about how to sell a screenplay.

But I didn't want to do any shoving. I wanted my agent to do the shoving, and hard! I wanted to build a long term relationship with Joel and all of the other Joels in Hollywood. Just as I didn't think it made any sense to sue the NFL to play in the league, I didn't think that any sign I was disrespectful in Hollywood could conceivably be to my benefit.

✱✱✱

The Summer 1997 issue of *Creative Screenwriting* carried an article by Steve Schlich entitled "Getting Attention in Hollywood." The article listed some of the methods to get a break in Hollywood, namely introductions, referrals, incredible talent, chance meetings, clever back door approaches, persistence, and even stalking. The overwhelmingly reliable way, the article went on to state, is to know someone who knows someone.

The same issue tallied the good news for those few who can get that elusive break: of the last 22 scripts sold, the average sales price was $479,000 "against" (the total, or balance, if it was produced) $938,000. Of the 22, nine were comedies. And script "doctors," the best ones, were hauling in $50,000 to $100,000 *a week* to rewrite someone else's stuff.

Fine by me.

The 1996 annual report of the Writers Guild reported that while some of these $1 million deals were truly being made, the Guild's 4,000 working members earned a median income of $84,608. This was less than I was making that year, but the chance to make 10 times that amount (and have more fun writing screenplays) was not something that I could even remotely hope for at my day job.

The creme de la creme among high-priced screenwriters in those days, Joe Eszterhas, was paid $4 million for *Showgirls*, and

M. Night Shyamalan sold *Unbreakable* for $5 million. In 2004, Terry Rossio and Bill Marsilii sold the screenplay for *Deja Vu* for $5 million. Lottery numbers.

✳✳✳

In early June, 1997 I received a short letter from Bryan Lourd with the copy of the Creative Artists Agency Submission Release which Terry Porter had sent with a copy of *Wheels* to Lourd's client, Joel Schumacher. On June 20, the theatrical opening day for *Batman and Robin*, I received a letter from Schumacher saying:

"Thank you for sending the information on your project *Wheels*. Although I found it to be interesting and original, it is not something for me at this time. Thank you for thinking of me."

Maybe I should have used the butter knife.

Chapter 10

Open-field Running

I never insisted in any way that the people who worked for me offer help in my quest to sell a screenplay. Their assistance, or lack of it, was never taken into consideration when their annual performance reviews were done, and it never impacted their salaries. Really. Trust me.

But help they did. Friend/employee/psychic Kat King introduced me to Warren Weideman, President of Harmony Entertainment. Harmony Holdings, through its five operating divisions, is the oldest and largest producer of television commercials and music videos. They have produced every type of TV commercial (including live action, animation and special effects) for virtually every major advertising agency in the country, and they also produce infomercials and Web sites.

When I met Warren in late 1996, his firm was about to produce a theatrical mystery movie—their first—with Showtime cable network called *The Inspectors*, about the high-tech U.S. Postal Inspection Service. Harmony, through its production unit called Park Avenue Productions, was embarking on a mission to develop unique marketing and production alliances among advertising agencies, their clients and programming. They were seeking to create synergistic deals much like the *Texaco Star Theatre* and the *GE Theatre* in the Golden Age of television. Today's Hallmark *Hall of Fame* is a current example.

Warren started his film marketing career in 1979 as a consultant for Columbia Pictures' *1941*. It was his idea to put John Belushi masks on 300 members of the Elko High School Marching Band for a pageant that drew seven minutes of network television coverage as a reward for such a quirky, creative idea!

I met Warren one evening in the lobby of the Sheraton/Universal City during a business trip to LA. Warren scanned my synopses before quickly pointing to *Wheels* as the one he thought had promise, since it was very topical and "cause-related." Positive halo effect for an advertising brand with which to associate. He pledged to keep *Wheels* in mind for a future project.

Kat King proved to be a much better friend and marketing manager than psychic. I wish she could have "divined" the MCI downsizing coming for all of us a year ahead of time! But, it sure was fun watching her read tarot cards.

***

My Dad was a semi-retired golfer-headhunter in 1997 when he received a letter from Jim Trahey asking for job placement advice. Trahey had had a career in various aspects of sports and entertainment marketing, and had recently completed a four-hour documentary on the Nixon Administration with fellow Atlantan John (Watergate) Ehrlichman. Ehrlichman's wife owned a fashionable restaurant in Atlanta. I inquired of Trahey whether he and/or Ehrlichman would have any interest in helping to sell or produce *CATV*, my political murder mystery. It was a stretch, but I felt it was worth pursuing. As a result, I learned that Trahey's daughter was a former script reader in the Turner movie empire. She liked *Scattered Seeds*. But in the end, there was no movement on either screenplay. Dead ends.

***

In Washington, DC in 1997, three women formed a company called Cause Celebre. Robin Brooks, Margery Kraus, and Alma Viator would act as "brokers" between celebrities and charitable causes. For example, a "Save The Chipmunks" group might be looking for a celebrity spokesperson, and Cause Celebre would find a chipmunk-concerned celebrity. The reverse was true, also— a celebrity who had a particular fondness for, say, elk, could be introduced to all sorts of elk-aware groups by Cause Celebre. Viator was the wife of former Congressman Ben Jones, the man who played "Cooter" on the *Dukes of Hazzard*. Armed once again with my letter from Georgia Senator Max Cleland, I solicited the help of Cause Celebre in brokering a deal for my script *Wheels*, linking me with a celebrity actor/director, a studio, and a wheelchair-related cause. My letter offered Cause Celebre a commission on the sale of my script.

They passed.

***

I learned that Bo Derek had a disabled stepson, and passed the lead on to Terry Porter for follow-up. Would Bo act in, direct, or produce *Wheels*? What did she think of the content and tone of the script?

She passed.

***

Around that time, I read in a newspaper of how David Letterman had tried in vain to get permission from an Atlanta orthodontist to show a picture of a gap-toothed young Julia Roberts. I tracked down the dentist, Dr. Ted Aspes, and offered him a commission to help get *Wheels* in front of Julia, hoping that the Georgia connection and Senator Max Cleland's letter would help. I received a call back from his son, Jason Aspes, who had just returned to Atlanta from Los Angeles, where he had worked in the film industry at New Line, among other companies. Planning to pursue an advertising career in Atlanta while writing scripts and looking for properties to develop himself, Jason volunteered to read my scripts and provide some help and guidance, including sending them to production company Zide Entertainment (*Jingle All the Way*).

Zide passed on my scripts in 1997.

When Julia Roberts won the Oscar for *Erin Brockovich* in 2001, it was reported that Dr. Aspes gave away free tubes of toothpaste to make good on a bet he had with Roberts!

***

MCI, in anticipation of the merger with WorldCom, "downsized" a huge number of employees in the prepaid phone card division, including all of my prepaid card promotion department, in October of 1997. Along with my six-figure salary went great stock-options and other generous benefits (ouch!). This was the fifth time in my career that I had been "rightsized," to use another term, by merger or some other sort of corporate consolidation; fortunately I had managed to bounce back into a better situation almost every time. I knew more about the forms at the unemployment office than the Government workers behind the counter. The new term I heard was "career challenged," which I am sure was coined by some human resource management geek who was trying to sell a book of new buzz phrases. So now *I* was challenged to sell only two products: me and my scripts.

Not so surprisingly in this Dilbert-like culture, shortly after being downsized by MCI, I read in a trade magazine that my departed-department had won the top award in the industry for the best prepaid phone card promotional marketing campaign of the year—a project for Mobil Oil and its NASCAR racing team. I was very proud of this accomplishment, won with great co-workers whose lives had suddenly become jumbled, as so many are these days in the workplace. Ironically, during my subsequent job interviews, it took extra effort on my part to explain to a prospective employer why a company such as MCI, which prides itself on its marketing ability, would want to eliminate an award-winning department as mine had been. Years later, everything would be explained about MCI/WorldCom in gory detail on the front pages.

Losing five jobs through no fault of my own was a humbling experience, one which had caught me off-guard, every time. One day, you and your department are winning accolades for topnotch work, and literally the next day you are handed an envelope with a letter of dismissal and a severance check (or no check). There are no guarantees in life—no one owes you a job—and this happened to me in very large and very small companies alike. If there is any career safety at all, it is in the belief in yourself and your own ability to persevere, and if there is any consolation, it is in the remembering you lost a job through no fault of your own. But anyway, your creditors don't care.

As painful as the loss of income and a derailed career can be, I always felt equal pain when the company that downsized me would eventually bring in a new top-level management team touting "new marketing approaches" and "revolutionary promotional strategies," which were nothing more than the same ideas generated by my marketing department years before.

The MCI cut reminded me of other times at the unemployment office, standing around and trading stories with other men and women, all six-figure-income performers with MBAs and the matching BMWs. Some guys would literally shake when they discussed how financially strapped they were, having leveraged their lives with houses, cars, and all the other amenities they couldn't afford now. And everyone spoke of marital tension.

One time in the parking lot I spotted a guy, hunched over the steering wheel of his car, crying. We knew each other only from the unemployment line. I gently knocked on the car window, and he asked me to sit inside the car with him, which I did for a while until he could calm down and drive home.

I would share with my group at the unemployment office my past experiences in white-collar downsizing: the time I worked at a telemarketing job in the morning and as a health club fitness instructor at night, while interviewing during the afternoons; or the time I bought a $3 watch at Kmart so that I could go to the pawn shop every third week and hock my good watch for food and gas money—until finally a paycheck came that allowed me to get the good watch out of hock by paying an exorbitant interest rate. While all this certainly had shock-value for my white-collar brethren, such facts of life were common to the blue-collar folks across the room. After sharing, I could see expressions on the faces of people telling me that either they could swallow their pride and do any job with dignity if it meant survival—or they still considered hourly, part-time work beneath themselves.

However, one aspect of getting back into the job market seemed universal among the downsized white-collar personnel, the fact that few employers wanted to hire overqualified executives at a lower-than-market pay rate, even if the company and the would-be employee were desperate to make a match. The reasoning was simple: the employer didn't want to hire someone at a salary much lower than he or she had received previously because such a person would continue to look for another job (on company time) at the pay scale previously enjoyed. Typically, employers didn't want to upset "standard" company pay scales and compensation packages by formulating individually-designed, creative, and imaginative incentive plans, which was and is unfortunate for many. This left the once high-paid executives with a few choices: (a) keep looking for a position of equal standing and salary, with or without a part-time job, (b) go into business for themselves, which brought with it a different set of risks and rewards, (c) parlay their experience into a sales job (if they weren't already sales people) where a pay-for-performance deal could be worked out, hopefully with a base salary or an advance against commission to get them started, (d) continue searching for an employer who would offer a full-time job, any job, however low the pay, and then hope to get, sooner than later, a better paying job or a raise so that future employers wouldn't discount previous, higher salary years, (e) retire early, (f) win the lottery, or (g) teach. Or sell a screenplay.

I had some interesting dialogues with companies that wanted to test my resolve and *loyalty* to stay with them for a long period of time. Conversations like this:

> INTERVIEWER: We want you to be here for a long time.
> ME: I feel the same way!
> INTERVIEWER: How can we be sure you'll be loyal and not quit?
> ME: How about a long-term, written contract?
> INTERVIEWER: No, then we can't fire or downsize you.
> ME: Put in the contract the reasons why I could be let go.
> INTERVIEWER: We may make up the reasons as we go.
> ME: How do you want me to prove my loyalty?
> INTERVIEWER: I dunno, but you didn't answer my question.
> ME: Huh?

Just as no one owes you a job, no one owes you a return to a standard of living you previously enjoyed. That's life. There are no guarantees. But any relationship in which loyalty goes only one way will not last.

I enjoyed something of a blessing every time I had to get an hourly part-time job. Although I usually encountered bosses and co-workers with fewer academic credentials and less general business experience than myself, they rooted for me. They pumped me up before I would leave work for the day to go out on an interview. Whether they were older or younger, they took pleasure in knowing that one day I would leave for something better, even though they would stay behind. They encouraged me not to abandon my dreams of screenwriting, even though the stress from job-hunting almost drained every ounce of strength from me. The consideration and compassion shown to me by these people, men and women whose names and faces have faded from my mind, were often greater than I found in corporate America. They were my angels.

∗∗∗

Almost two-months after the MCI downsizing, in November of 1997, I joined the San Diego-based Fantastic Sports, Inc., a sports promotion agency, as a Vice President. The owner of the company, Fred Mort, knew the people at Mandalay Films (Peter Guber et al), and pledged to make some inquires for me. Fred's motto: "Pursue your dreams."

"Mort," from Latin, means death, and it was an omen: a year and a half later, after yet another merger situation, Mort downsized me for my sixth time by selling his company. The new company didn't need me or any of the current employees of Fantastic Sports, Inc. No severance check.

Every time after I took a new job, my name appeared in a trade publication announcing this blessed event, and a stream of cold-calling stockbrokers would hound me, expecting to come upon a new client with a windfall of loose cash to spread around. Following the MCI debacle, when I informed them that I had been downsized five times in my life, and each time had to liquidate stock and 401K assets just to put food on the table, they hung up the phone faster than I did. I was still getting such broker calls literally on my last day at Fantastic Sports.

∗∗∗

My friend Gregg Gerstman has a cousin, Scott Greenstein, who was Senior Vice President of the Motion Picture Group at Miramax in 1997, and I had Terry Porter send him all my script synopses. The reply from an assistant to Greenstein was that they liked *Wheels*, but wouldn't commit until major talent was "attached." This left Porter in a Catch-22, but not without a lead because Terry had met with Bill Murray's agent at Creative Artists

Agency. However, from them we got the same answer: If Miramax is in, and will pay the price, sure, Murray's in. No one would commit first. Catch-22. Like sand running though one's fingers, just out of grip.

While Gregg continued to lobby Greenstein at family dinners, he met Kathleen Thomas on a plane. Thomas was in charge of development at New York-based Longfellow Pictures (*Prince of Tides*). Like almost everyone else, her first choice when she read about my work was to look at *Wheels*.

She then sent *Wheels* out for "coverage"—a trade term used for a reader who breaks down the script into various areas such as characters, plot, cost, etc., resulting in an overall rating (i.e., should we buy it or not). The "cover notes" Thomas received indicated that *Wheels* was "one of the best comedies" and "one of the most well-written" scripts ever read by the studio. Kathleen, with her hectic schedule as head of development and her myriad other studio responsibilities, was finding it hard to find time to read *Wheels* herself. So, I sent her two gift certificates for New York's Peninsula Hotel's spa—one for her to use for a massage and facial while she read the script, and one for her coverage reader as a "thank you." She replied that she couldn't accept the gifts because of ethical rules, which I appreciated. (I resold the spa certificates at a discount to Gregg Gerstman for his mom.)

Eventually Kathleen Thomas did read *Wheels*, though Longfellow Pictures then passed because the script "wasn't exactly what they needed" at that time.

But, on the strength of that reading, Kathleen requested synopses of my other scripts. The next one she asked to have covered was *CATV*, my cable TV murder mystery. Again, it came back with high marks from the coverage readers, and she promised to read it herself and make the ultimate determination.

Conversation with Thomas:

THOMAS: The coverage was again excellent! I'm going to read it.

ME: (a little surprised) Uh, thanks ... very much.

THOMAS: You seem a little surprised.

ME: (a little surprised) Uh, well, yeah ... and grateful.

THOMAS: Brad, listen, I think you may be underestimating yourself. Really. Every year, we spot two good first-time writers that we know are going to make it. This year, I think you might be one of those two! It'll happen for you.

ME: (stunned) Uh, thanks. Very much.

THOMAS: Maybe *CATV* will be our first project together!

ME: (stunned) Uh, thanks. Very much.

THOMAS: I'm going to read it soon.

ME: (stunned) Uh, thanks. Very much.

That conversation with Kathleen Thomas made up for hundreds of rejections. That glimmer of hope was more than enough to keep me going. "I think you may be underestimating yourself," she had said.

Almost with a tear in my eye, I related that Kathleen Thomas' quote to Darrah. Her own quote, sure to bring me down to earth: "Show me the money, honey!" This was also fast becoming the first understandable sentence of my son Andy, now age 2. If I lived long enough, *he* might be my next agent.

Kathleen left Longfellow Pictures shortly afterwards for another job in Los Angeles, and I lost track of her. Years later when I finally found her, she was out of the film business and out of touch with previous entertainment industry people. Yet, she was still supportive. "Don't quit, Brad."

✳✳✳

In response to a query I sent to the Writers Guild, I received from Christopher Dexter, the Agency Administrator, an outline of the screening process by which an agency can become a real live signatory of the Guild. The "very strict screening process" includes providing a copy of the agency's business license, a sample contract, a letter printed on letterhead which promises that the agency will not represent its own employees, a copy of an agency's phone bill, a voided trust account check, and a signed Artists Management Agreement. Give the Guild all that and you're in. But, if you then do something unethical, you can get kicked out.

My original question had been answered: becoming an agent was tougher than getting a fishing license. There are only about 500 agencies in the U.S. listed as Writers Guild signatories, each of which employs from one to over a hundred individual agents.

My agent, Terry Porter from little Flat Rock, Indiana, had worked so hard during the first nine months of our agreement that I committed to another year with him, to run from August 1, 1997 to July 31, 1998, and after that committed to another extension. He had sent me regular status reports of his correspondence and meetings with agencies and producers, concentrating on *Wheels, North Wind,* and *Cleaning Up.* No sales yet. But his personal pitch meetings in LA with Steven Spielberg and others were enough to tell me that he had more than just an LA phonebook and casual industry contacts. He was mining deep relationships formed over a long time.

Ted Baehr was helping Terry with some introductions, as he thought *Wheels* and *North Wind* were high concept, high-moral-value scripts. I finally was able to meet with Dr. Ted in late August 1998, as he came through Atlanta (having relocated to Los Angeles) to promote his latest book, *The Media-Wise Family,* a guide for parents in counseling their children about entertainment selections. We met for a brief lunch, and Ted gave me a *North Wind* endorsement quote to include in pitches to studios, producers and agents, as well as to include in press releases to media outlets, all in hopes of generating some "buzz" for screenplays which were never assured of seeing the light of day. Ted said of *North Wind* that it "…picks up where *Braveheart* left off … a haunting, powerful epic about personal freedom and eternal values." Would this strong quote help me get noticed and differentiate my work from that of other wannabe writers?

✳✳✳

Since the screenwriting award from the Charleston International Film Festival for *Wheels* was continuing to open doors for me, I thought I'd give competition another try. One of the more prestigious is the Academy Foundation (as in *the* Academy Awards) Nicholl Fellowships, five $25,000 awards that ensure a ton of positive press and valuable contacts. I entered the 1997 contest with *Scattered Seeds*, *Wheels*, *Cleaning Up*, *CATV*, and *Brothers' Brunch*. I would have liked to enter *North Wind*, but (then) at only 85 pages, it was too short for their competition requirements. The entry fee was $30 each.

Past winners of the Nicholl included Randy McCormick (*Speed 2*), Andrew Marlowe (*Air Force One*), and Susannah Grant (*Pocohontas*, fifteen episodes of Fox's *Party of Five*). Good writers. Tough competition.

The envelope, please.

The rejection letter for all of my entries stated that the 1997 competition drew 4006 entries, and that judging is "inherently both a personal and an extremely subjective matter … (and that) lack of success here may have little bearing on your placement in other competitions or in the marketplace where a sale is the ultimate measure of success."

The next competition I entered in 1997, The Writer's Network Screenplay & Fiction Competition, netted me a quarter finalist notice for both *Wheels* and *North Wind*. Out of 2,452 screenplay entries, I made the cut to 734, before not making the next cut to 159.

Subjective indeed.

*** * * *

Father Methodius, the business manager monk of the Monastery of the Holy Spirit, located in Conyers, a small town south of Atlanta, was the recipient of a letter from me inquiring if he would endorse *North Wind* in return for a donation of the sale of the script. The monastery made money by accepting donations from those seeking retreat at their dormitory, and by selling stained glass, hay from their 1000 acres under cultivation, and gift shop items. The Monastery was in need of funds, said a recent newspaper account.

Perhaps Fr. Methodius and the community of monks would feel a kinship with the historic monks of the European monasteries that were raided by the Vikings? He did, and the monastery agreed to endorse the script for a 10% commission. So, in January, 1998, I began drafting the press release while Terry Porter and his partner Dave Ruiz set about organizing a press conference at the monastery to announce the unprecedented partnership of a screenwriter and a community of monks.

* * *

I answered an ad in a November, 1997, *Variety* for scripts, placed by a producer in Australia. I decided to invest over $100 to send him my package via UPS from Atlanta, including a copy of *North Wind*, and as a gift, a replica of a Viking chess board.

I never heard back from him. Nothing ventured, nothing gained.

* * *

In November of 1997, the promotion agency where I worked was engaged in the hottest thing of the moment, the Internet. I spent a great deal of time surfing the net for, and on behalf of, clients, and in between clicks for my day job, my search sometimes wandered over into the screenplay arena. By inputting words into the search engine such as "Hollywood," "independent producer," "seeking screenplays," "screenplay submissions," and others, in various combinations, I was able to uncover a handful of small independents who were accepting screenplay submissions after an e-mail query to gain permission. No need to involve Terry Porter in these—the web sites had their own waiver/release form to download, sign, and send in.

While surfing one day, I came across Francis Ford Coppola's American Zoetrope motion picture web site. The large type on the screen suddenly read, "Welcome to the American Zoetrope Screenplay Submissions Site. American Zoetrope now accepts submissions of feature-length screenplays over the Internet." This was by far the largest and most prestigious film company I had found that did so.

The next paragraph on the web site detailed the submission policy:

"For each screenplay that you submit we ask that you read and review four screenplays submitted by other screenwriters. The screenplays you submit will in turn be read and reviewed by others. American Zoetrope staff, who are always looking for good new screenplays to produce, will read the best-received screenplays. As a participant you will receive the benefit of seeing your work reviewed and discussed by a diverse group of writers from all over the world."

What?!

They expect me to read other screenwriters' works and "grade" them as being worthy or not of production—perhaps ahead of my own screenplays? Huh?

Look, I don't mind helping anyone. But this is a competitive marketplace, and I for one believed that my scripts were as good or better than anything else out there, or I wouldn't show them at all. At least that was my belief, to be proved right or wrong by the marketplace, subjective or not, not by a collaborative effort in which through some writer group-think the best scripts are selected. Other studios hired (i.e., paid real money to) "coverage" people to obtain a somewhat objective opinion. I wasn't on Zoetrope's payroll.

I was willing to give up large percentages of my script sales to benefit worthy causes. But other than that, there was only one Golden Rule in Hollywood: the studios with the Gold make the Rules, and those rules say that no one's opinion counts except theirs. I accept that wholeheartedly, I guess because I've lived so long with the "bottom line" thinking of the competitive business world. But what a ridiculous proposition this was.

***

Ted Baehr had shared *North Wind* with producer/director Mike Rhodes whose credits included feature films such as *Dorothy Day, Romero*, and *The Bus is Coming*. He had been nominated for a Golden Globe for the miniseries *Heidi* for which he won both the New York International Film Festival Award and the Catholics in Media Award. His TV movies included *Runaway Car* and *Not our Son*, and on TV he also directed the series *Christy*, Humanitas Prize-winning episodes for *China Beach*, *Equal Justice*, *A Year in the Life*, and, as out of sync as it may at first appear, *Baywatch*. He was a past winner of Baehr's Templeton Awards.

Rhodes called me with some feedback after reading *North Wind*. We talked for an hour. Mike had great ideas for improving the plot and character development. He wondered aloud if Sean Connery was right for the lead role. As we spoke in March of 1998, during the week leading up to the Oscar awards, Rhodes said he would be very interested in directing *North Wind*, and would use it in his upcoming studio pitches. (Viking women in *Baywatch* bikinis? I hoped not.)

A few days before the 1998 Oscars, I also received a Beverly Hills postcard from Terry Porter who was in LA to pitch scripts and meet with Rhodes. Was this finally the last stage leading up to a big development deal for me?

***

Terry Porter admitted that publicity was not a strength his agency possessed. Communication with media people for the purpose of getting stories placed was a different discipline, and a different set of contacts, than pitching studio producers about scripts. Terry encouraged me to find a publicist who would be able to place stories about the endorsements I had received from Senator Cleland and the Monastery. Once stories were placed, the plan was, Terry could walk into a studio and say, "Hey, look at the unique publicity my unknown screenwriter is pulling down ... better grab his scripts now before someone else capitalizes on the 'heat' from the pre-production publicity"—or something like that. Hype.

I figured if the woman from Iowa with the two-headed frog was getting coverage in popular magazines and 15 seconds on the nightly news, then endorsement stories about my scripts should at least get me a mention, right? No one other than me, as far as I knew, had done this quirky stuff.

I surfed the Internet (search words: "Hollywood Publicists") and found a few publicists to whom I sent e-mail. Jeannie Berg sent an eager reply. Jeannie had moved to Glendale, Arizona, from Los Angeles where she had amassed impressive credentials including work in the Warner Brothers feature film publicity office. I hired Jeannie for an initial $750, which would pay for pitches of press releases about two different endorsements:

- Max Cleland and Award from Charleston International Film Festival (*Wheels*)
- The Monastery of the Holy Spirit (*North Wind*)

After that initial effort, she charged $45 an hour plus 50% of the expenses. In August, 1998, we agreed on contract terms that specified she could work up to 10 hours a month, with extra hours worked only with my approval. A Georgia-based screenwriter, I now had a Hollywood agent in Indiana and a Hollywood publicist in Arizona. My "virtual Hollywoodland" was stretching out. But, hey, it was the "virtual technology '90s", and it seemed to fit right in.

I heard back from one other entertainment publicist, Jack McAdoo of PubliStar in Clearwater, Florida. Jack said that rather than propose his publicity services, he got so excited about my script endorsements that he requested and received from me copies of *Wheels*, *North Wind*, and *Scattered Seeds*, and sent them to his contacts at Century Films. In mid-August, 1998, Century was lining up projects for the next two years, and their initial reaction was that they liked all of my scripts:

> JACK: Initial reaction is that they liked all of your scripts!
> ME: Huh?
> JACK: Your scripts are on a short list for selection.
> ME: How short?
> JACK: Very short.
> ME: Can you be more specific?
> JACK: Very, very, short!
> ME: Do I pay you and my current agent a double
>   commission?
> JACK: I would work out a deal with your agent. Probably
>   split the 10%.

I'm still waiting to hear back from Jack.

***

A pattern was beginning to emerge. Trying to sell a screenplay was a form of controlled chaos. Sure, it had boundaries, but within those boundaries, there was no single way to reach the goal. Personal relationships, networking, film festivals, film school alliances, self-production, agencies, dumb luck—none insured success by themselves, but each alone or in various combinations could provide an avenue. Each player had a role, but the roles could change quickly, depending on the situation. People could help you along for a part of the way, but then another person had to take over the task. This pattern had many of the characteristics of my life in the business world, but there was something else. Something more. Something more special about this feeling.

Where had I seen this situation before? It was familiar, this drive toward a goal which required agility, flexibility, and a sense of urgency. Where? And then it came to me.

Football!

Running with a football, particularly one which has been punted, kicked, or passed to you, requires what is known as open-field running. There are eleven opposing players, each of whom has only the desire to remove your head from your shoulders. But they don't know which way you are going to run because you don't know where you are going to run! Your teammates don't know where you are going. You live second to second. There are boundaries and rules, sure. But the path from where you began, to where you want to go—the endzone—is anything but straight. Or assured. You are in the open field.

The best open-field runner of all time was Chicago Bear Gale Sayers. Watch the movie *Brian's Song* sometime, and you will see actual footage of him on the football field. His nickname was "Magic," and you will see why.

There are choices to be made. Do I run here, or there? How much effort expended to go here, or there? Who can help me if I follow them? Who really doesn't give a damn and wouldn't help his own mother? What are the obstacles, seen and unforeseen? Am I good enough on this day? Any day?

But you can't stop to think. You can't stop at all. Each action produces a reaction. Each reaction another action. Fake left, go right. The field, and the players on it, look different from second to second. They have moved and so have you. What worked a second ago, or a year ago, may not work now. You just have to trust and act, and hope the hard work you have done, and your instinct and some luck, will pay off.

That's open-field running. That's writing and selling a screen-play. Controlled chaos. Open-field running with a football in hand is one of the most exhilarating and liberating feelings I have ever felt. Particularly if it ends in a touchdown.

These days, when I have run too far, or jogged at more than a 10-minute per mile pace, I often feel a slight twinge of pain in my right hamstring which I injured decades before while training for professional football. The pain never lingers longer than a couple minutes, and somehow, it makes me smile as one would if seeing an old friend after a long absence.

When I jog now, always slowly, I think of times when I ran fast in the open field. Alone, just listening to my own breathing as my feet shuffle along, I let my imagination run wild. And in those times, stories come to me. I'm in the open field again.

How close to the Hollywood goal would my open-field run-ning take me?

Chapter 11

Who Are You?

My favorite movie of all time is *The Wizard of Oz*. Naturally, my son Andy is exposed to it a lot. One morning in early September, 1998, while I was shaving and he was watching the *Oz* video, my 3-year old ran into the bathroom and parroted the phrase of the Wizard: "Who are you?! Who are you?!" He laughed and darted out, and I was left staring at myself in the mirror, pondering the question.

The press kit went out from Jeannie Berg in late September. There were two versions of the press releases, each containing the same information, but with slightly different emphases.

Entitled "Screenwriter Inks His Own Deals" and "A Screenwriter's Journey of Faith," both two-page releases were accompanied by a two-page biography which thematically linked my academic, marketing, sports, and screenwriting careers, as well as my being a Dad to Andy. There were no head shots, because aside from the extra expense, we figured that if someone wanted pictures, they would send their own photographer. (I scouted nearby tanning bed salon locations just in case.)

The releases recounted the *North Wind* endorsement from the Monastery in return for a 10% donation. Father Methodius was quoted as saying, "The Holy Spirit Abbey is proud to participate in helping to bring this story to the screen. We feel a close kinship with our Brothers, those monks who faced adversity in that time in history, many centuries ago. Their unyielding faith is our heritage, our common bond through the ages." The releases included Dr. Ted's previous quote comparing *North Wind* to *Braveheart*.

The presentation of *Wheels* included the Senator Cleland endorsement, quoting from his 1993 letter that the script offered "a hopeful and insightful approach to humanity … (I)n a world that has proven tragedy, this story suggests that there are happy endings if you believe in the philosophy that life is what you make of it." The donation to each of the Christopher Reeve Foundation to Cure Paralysis, Momentum International, and the U.S. Paralympic Committee from the sale of the script was noted.

Jeannie ended one press release with:

"Catherman's themes of courage, hope, endurance, and faith are omnipresent in his writing and his quest to get his screenplays on the big screen. Stories have been written of men and women who possess the kind of enthusiasm, talent, creativity, and pure tenacity found in Catherman. It's only a matter of time before his unique and fascinating story will be told."

Jeannie ended the other press release with:

"Catherman's passion for his work and enterprising ways are not unusual in our time of everyday heroes like John Glenn and Ted Turner. What makes this man stand out is the fact that he's undaunted by the immense challenges that he faces as an artist in getting his work produced, and the pure bravado and ingenuity that he employs to meet those challenges. It appears evident that Catherman is the stuff of which Hollywood movies are made."

The release was peppered with the names of some of the people to whom Porter had submitted the script, or at least would by the time the release was out: Ron Howard, Schwarzenegger, Costner, Spielberg, Reeve, Joel Silver, Ron Bass, and the Cario/Simpson team. We phrased such references carefully so as not to imply that these celebrities had endorsed the scripts, let alone made an offer to buy any of them. (This would be important later.)

Our hope was that taken together, the releases, rather than being exploitative, would position the endorsements to become an extension of the enthusiasm and creativity of the author. In fact, the release clearly stated that the reason for my acquiring the endorsements was to "gain the respect from people or organizations who are close enough to the subject matter to let me know, and let potential producers know, that I had written the stories in an honest, truthful manner." At least that part of the release was true.

The release was sent to thirty media outlets, including *Variety* and other trade journals, consumer magazines such as *Entertainment Weekly*, and electronic press such as CNN (I knew no one on the editorial side, even though I had worked there in marketing). My hometown paper, the *Atlanta Journal-Constitution*, was an obvious target. Terry Porter sent releases to those contacts who had requested at least one script in the past. I sent a release, anonymously in a plain envelope, to each of the Board Members of the Christopher Reeve Foundation, including Marsha and Robin Williams, in care of the Foundation's address listed on its web site. The only contact name and phone number contained in the release was that of Jeannie Berg and her company, Illuminata Communications, which added a measure of professionalism and apparent objectivity.

I rummaged through my old files for names of producers and practically anyone else who had requested a script over the years. They each got a press release. I faxed a copy to Senator Cleland's office in Washington in case he was questioned. I promptly received a reply from Cleland: "Congratulations ... thank you for keeping me updated ... it was great to hear from you ... best wishes and good luck."

After a brief discussion with head of the United States Paralympic Committee, Mark Shepherd, I faxed him a copy of the release. He thanked me for my potential donation, and cautioned me not to use unauthorized wheelchair racing film footage in the movie until licensing rights could be negotiated.

I sent Ted Baehr a letter of thanks for taking time from his busy schedule to meet with me and give me a quote for my release. My letter was published in the October, 1998, issue of his *Movieguide Magazine*. In that same issue, Ms. Terri Tingle, a Senior Vice President of Public Affairs for Turner Entertainment based in Atlanta, also had a letter published in which she congratulated Ted on his recent book. I sent Tingle a press release. Could she help me network though the Turner organization? Could I get a meeting since we were both in Atlanta? She never replied.

Our first response came in the form of a letter to Jeannie dated October 5, 1998, from Joel M. Faden, Treasurer of the Christopher Reeve Foundation. This response was prompted by one of the anonymous press releases I had sent to the Board members of Reeve's group. The letter began by thanking me for the potential donation upon the sale of *Wheels*, but ended by asking us not to use the name of Reeve or the Foundation in a way that implied an endorsement "unless and until such time that Mr. Reeve or we have agreed to any involvement in writing." The letter copied Reeve and Robert Solomon, the Foundation's legal counsel.

The middle paragraph of Faden's letter referenced the fact that Reeve's "assistant (had already) returned the script to Mr. Catherman." However, Terry Porter still decided to pursue Reeve through persons whom he felt would have influence on Reeve to reconsider. According to Porter, his friend director Ken Wales (*Christy*) had been attempting to pitch *Wheels* to Reeve for the better part of a year without success, but was still trying because Wales believed so much in the script.

No reconsideration ever happened.

✳✳✳

Bill Higgins, in an article entitled "Rejected Scripts Finally Make Stage Appearance" for the October 12, 1998, issue of *Vari-*

ety, told the funny story (depending on your perspective) of how Andrew Gaty was staging the play *The Sun Dialogues* about a studio reader who rejects 1000 scripts. For props, Gaty put out a call to friends, agencies, and the Writers Guild for rejected scripts: he needed 1000 but quickly received 10,000! I'm sure several of mine made the pile. Said Gaty about the sheer number of rejections, "You really wonder what your future is." No kidding.

That same week in October, Jeannie Berg informed me she had to terminate our three-month agreement on November 15, 1998, because she had been hired to rewrite an independently produced comedy. She also informed me in mid-October that *Symbol Magazine*, which covered the culture of Atlanta and the South, had committed to do an article about me and those quirky endorsements. The magazine was requesting photographs to review. A break!

Symbol at that time had a paid circulation of 105,000 in major cities of the Carolinas, Georgia, Tennessee, Florida, and Alabama. The targeted readership was between 30 and 50 years of age, with an average age of 44, and an average income of $107,000. The extent of readership among movie producers was unknown, but by my guess, zero.

I quickly had to get professional photographs. No time for the tanning bed, although I had never been in one. I found a photography studio in the phone book advertising one-day-turn-around head shots. At the studio, after a couple test shots, it soon became apparent that my glasses caused too much glare in the photographs. I had tried contact lenses a few years before, and had used them exactly three times before giving up. (In Hell, you spend all day putting in and taking out contact lenses, and I'm sure that the relevant Bible verse was lost somewhere, somehow.) So, for times like this, the photographer had a table of eyeglass props *without* the glass in them. I matched my own pair as closely as I could, and we began shooting.

The "contact sheet," as it is called, had 26 shots the size of those small ones you get in 4-for-$1 booths at the mall or airport, all arranged in columns on an 8 ½" x 11" black-and-white glossy sheet. I sent the sheet, per Jeannie's instructions, to the Managing Editor of *Symbol*, Jane G. Gaston. I received an e-mail reply from Gaston in late October specifying the three shots she wanted to see blown-up to 5" x 7" black-and-white glossies, and telling me Mr. Jeff Kent, on assignment in France at the time, would be the editor assigned to do my interview, and write the piece.

The three shots I made into 5" x 7"s presented an interesting mix. The first had me propping my smiling face on my right fist, with the sleeve of my white-collared starched shirt rolled-up. This shot said, "Hi, I'm a kinda happy-and-friendly-guy, just taking life as it comes while I make a fool of myself, and gee-whiz, I'd sure like to sell a screenplay."

The second shot had me resting my chin on my folded white-shirted arms, with a hint of a wry smile which said, "Look, I'm an angst-ridden-artist-suffering-for-my-art-kind-of-guy, and I'm in a blue period because my genius hasn't been discovered yet, and I'm vulnerable and very sensitive at this moment, so be careful what you say around me, will ya?—or I might start to cry."

The third was a mid-chestline frontal shot, with the body leaning into the frame, of me wearing a blue blazer and white open collar shirt, smiling, which said, "Next up, all the day's sports action and scores after we return from this commercial break!" I looked like a sportscaster. There were bald spots on my temple I hadn't noticed before. Must have been the lighting.

I'm glad they didn't pick the one where I'm leaning on my elbows with both open palms pressed against my cheeks. I looked liked Milton Berle.

The last week of October, 1998, I also sent my usual quarterly check to Terry Porter in the amount of $75. I had just ended two years and three months with him as my agent without realizing my first sale or even an option. If the article in *Symbol* did not somehow spur some action, I told myself, I was going to mail reprints of the article to other agencies to find a different agent—one, hopefully, based in Los Angeles.

In mid-November, Steven Spielberg was awarded the 1998 Catholics in Media motion picture award for *Saving Private Ryan*. In 1994, *Schindler's List* won the same award. In accepting the award before 500 people at the Beverly Hilton Hotel, Spielberg said, "What's important for all of us who make films is to respect our audience with taste and integrity, and with ideas and ideals."

What was Spielberg thinking about *North Wind*? Was he still thinking about it at all? Was it still "under consideration" by DreamWorks, as Porter believed? With a recent production management shuffle at DreamWorks, had my script been successfully passed along, or did it die when the new manager took over?

Jeff Kent, the writer for *Symbol*, contacted me to set up a date for the interview, to be held in his office. By that morning of November 16, I had not received a confirming letter from Porter or from any producer, let alone Spielberg or Reeve, confirming that any of my scripts were still "under consideration." Nor did Porter have an official letter of "commitment" from director Mike Rhodes.

Jeff Kent flipped on the tape recorder and we began the interview, which was to last for an hour and a half. It was electrifying for me. We agreed that he would give me a future deadline for inclusion of names of specific producers who were "actively" considering my work. Terry Porter was thus given a reprieve to get busy and get some letters out, and answers back in.

I outlined for Kent what I thought was a good theme for the article when he asked what the common thread was running from my marketing career to my would-be screenwriting career. I said that in essence I was a "storyteller." When a client has a product for me to market, I develop a story to tell consumers; I tell stories through screenplays; I tell my little boy Andy a story at bedtime.

When he asked why I wrote at all, I quoted Rod Steiger who said about acting that the only answer is "I have to do it … not because I want to … but, to feel alive … to feel whole." The act of creating for its own sake was a reward that had sustained me for years without a sale.

When asked if I ever got depressed during the years without making a sale, I answered that my knee-jerk reaction to rejection was to get back into action, and that small victories count. Then I told him about my open-field running analogy.

✳✳✳

While waiting for the *Symbol* article to come out, and for Porter to use the press release both to spur sales and to obtain letters of "interest" for the magazine article, I continued to surf the Internet as well as the classified ads in *Variety* and *The Hollywood Reporter* in search of independent producers seeking screenplays. In early December, I logged on to www.hollydex.com and found Straw Hut Entertainment, a Hilton Head, South Carolina-based movie producer advertising for:

"…moving events, reason for existence tales in any genre that can be produced in the $3 to $10 million range. Please submit a treatment via e-mail and we will get back to you should we become interested."

I e-mailed synopses of all my scripts, along with a summary of the endorsements I had received. The next day, Joe Rowland of Straw Hut requested scripts, and I sent him *North Wind, Wheels,* and *Scattered Seeds,* the press release and bio written by Jeannie Berg, and synopses of my other scripts. Joe was the 27-year old head of Straw Hut Entertainment, a multimedia and film production company with a growing corporate client and production services roster. They were looking for their first big movie production.

Joe's financial backer for movies was Marlene Mendoza, whom he had met through business connections of his family. Joe had a few projects in development with Mendoza at the time I sent my e-mail. Surfing the net again, I found Mendoza's resume which was outstanding. Born in 1952 in Montreal, she made an impressive string of career moves in the 1970s and early 1980s in banking and finance, was a world traveler, and studied for six years at La Verne University in California. In the late 1980s, her MMMM and Associates engaged in a variety of small entrepreneurial business investments, including some work in independent film production.

On May 15, 1990, Mendoza formed Film Capital Corporation, a company dedicated to motion picture finance from overseas investment. She had amassed a war chest in excess of $100 million for film financing. (Really?!) Her own first production was listed on her web site as *Hello Puberty*, a comedy scheduled to shoot in 1999 through her Emerald Cinema Productions, in association with executive producer Charles B. Wessler (*There's Something About Mary*).

A flurry of phone calls and e-mails continued between Joe and myself for several days while he read. Although he received hundreds of scripts on a regular basis, my endorsement along with the directing "interest" of Mike Rhodes had pushed my scripts to the top of the pile! My Cause Marketing angle had worked. After reading, and reading only *North Wind*, Joe consulted with Mendoza and they were ready to offer me an Option Agreement! Here was my first big break, thought I.

Joe first questioned the length of *North Wind* which was only 70 pages. When I told him that the script had "lost" some pages because of a formatting change recommended to me by another producer, Joe instructed me to reformat the script the previous way. After I added no more than six pages, we agreed that the script was full-length (at least two hours of film), as Mike Rhodes and others had said previously (this becomes important later, as the reader will note). Unlike my script *Wheels*, a comedy filled with snappy dialogue that required lots of pages, *North Wind* was a script that included lengthy action descriptions in long paragraph form.

I brought Joe Rowland and Terry Porter together, and they had a brief introductory talk before Joe faxed Terry and me an Option Agreement contract on December 16, 1998. The Agreement called for payment of $1 to me to secure for Straw Hut an exclusive option from December 16, 1998 until June 16, 1999. Then, if Straw Hut wished to continue the option, they could pay an additional dollar for sole option rights until December 16, 1999. The next clause stated that if Straw Hut exercised their option to purchase and produce *North Wind*, they would then pay me $500,000 in a lump sum. This payment did not include any services of mine to do rewrites, which would come under a separate contract *if* they wanted to hire me to do the rewrites at all.

Another clause in the contract called for me to receive 2% of the profits from domestic and international distribution, video sales, and merchandising after recouping all expenses for production, exhibition, and marketing. Net profit, not gross, in addition to the $500,000 lump sum.

Given that *North Wind* had languished in several hands at DreamWorks by that time, and that no other offer was close to consummation, Terry and I agreed to accept the contract. Terry's first thought was that the option price should be 10% of the sales price, i.e., $50,000, but we didn't feel comfortable enough with our leverage at that point to press the case. We decided to take the buck.

Terry stood to make $50,000 as his 10% commission on $500,000, and even though I found the Straw Hut lead and he didn't, his counsel and help with the expected second "rewrite services" contract would be invaluable. In addition, in my mind, he had earned his money bringing Mike Rhodes to the project through Ted Baehr. And, hopefully with this sale, other offers would come from new and existing contacts of his. Since the Monastery would also get $50,000 as per my pledge to them, I would have a $400,000 payday for my first script sale.

SOLD! I signed the contract and sent it back to Joe on Friday, December 18. In fact, upon Joe's insistence, I drove back to the office on that Friday evening to fax the Option contract so that he could "instruct his awaiting team" to start that very night to work on the storyboards and budget. Joe informed me that, although I hadn't realized it, I had just "wrecked some holidays" for those of his team who would be working diligently night and day through Christmas and New Year's to get the materials ready for Mendoza.

I e-mailed Jeff Kent at *Symbol* with the news in hopes that he could put an addendum into his article, then scheduled to be in the March issue.

I forgot to ask Joe to sign a dollar bill and send it to me so I could frame it—as I had tried to do with Jason Hervey when he optioned *Wheels* for the same princely sum. With my luck, I envisioned my Hollywood nickname would become "Dollar Bill" or "Buck." But maybe my luck was changing. Luck? Maybe during this Christmas season, my monks down at the Monastery had put in some extra prayers as they had promised they would!

Joe was excited to begin his next step in the production process, which included securing talent interest, and then budgeting the script. Armed with talent, a brief storyboard of the key plot elements, a firm budget, a commitment from Mike Rhodes to direct, a planned hiring of Dr. Ted Baehr as a consultant, and the longer synopsis I would write, Mendoza would then "shop" the package to the major studios in hopes of securing a distribution deal. The initial guess from Joe and Mendoza was that the production alone, aside from distribution and marketing, would cost more than $50 million, which would come from Mendoza's company, while an equal amount would be sought from a studio for marketing and distribution. *North Wind* would be expensive to make.

Darrah was excited, no matter how much she tried to hide her joy:

DARRAH: How much?!
ME: One dollar … but, if …
DARRAH: Let me see the dollar first.

I thought Andy would be an easier target for some attention:

ME: Daddy's gonna make a movie!
ANDY: Like a video?
ME: Well, yeah, we can watch the video of Daddy's movie.
ANDY: Daddy, can you go to the car and get it now?
ME: Never mind. Eat your dinner.

Without thinking, one of my first reactions was to call my Dad and share the good news. Then the irony and significance of the moment hit me, coming as it did the week before Christmas. Because of my Dad's death just five months before, *North Wind* had new meaning for me. The script concerned a Viking chieftain and his father, a Viking chieftain and his son, and a monk who has a figurative (holy) father. Each father tried to pass along his values and beliefs as best he could, while guiding, directing, loving, disciplining, and otherwise molding character, which would in turn be passed on from generation to generation.

I reached over and hugged my son.

On New Year's Day, 1999, I received a voicemail from Joe Rowland telling me that he had had "good preliminary discussions" with both director Mike Rhodes and Dr. Ted Baehr about moving the project forward. No word yet about my writing a new two-page synopsis for the sales package that Rowland and Mendoza would be pitching to a studio/distributor.

In early January, I did, however, receive my check for $1 from Straw Hut Entertainment. In addition to Hilton Head, Straw Hut had an office in Savannah, Georgia, a short distance away. It was on their bank account in Savannah that my check was drawn, although "Strawhut" was condensed to one word on the check, which I found a little odd. I had the uncashed check framed, and mounted it over my computer. My first payment as a screenwriter had been received.

I sent Terry Porter a dime to cover his 10% commission. The custom framing of the check, with tax, cost $30.99.

✳✳✳

In late January, I discovered The Viking Heritage on the Internet (www.Viking.hgo.se), an organization which was a part of Gotland University in Sweden. For 150 SEK ($23 US), I bought a membership that included a book and a newsletter. In addition to publishing the newsletter, The Viking Heritage held conferences and seminars, and generally "enhanced understanding of Viking history, operating at both international and national levels."

In early February, I received confirmation of my membership and was issued "Honoured Member/Subscriber" number 361. The newsletter told of shipbuilding recreations, excavations of Viking sites, and a new Stockholm tourist attraction called "Vikingaliv" (World of the Vikings), set to open in 2002. This theme park would cover 4500 square meters and expected 800,000 visits from tourists a year. It would offer Viking cuisine in its restaurants, and would present various multimedia shows. Its opening would co-incide with Stockholm's 750-year jubilee. It seemed Vikings were being rediscovered the world over, just as I had predicted years before.

Cool.

The February, 1999 issue of *Creative Screenwriting Magazine* mentioned the sale of another Viking screenplay entitled *The Last Viking*. Script treatment was by the late Calder Willingham (*One-Eyed Jacks, The Graduate, Rambling Rose, Little Big Man*), fleshed out by Charles Pogue (*The Fly, Braveheart*). Fox 2000 executive producer Laura Ziskin, whose credits included *No Way Out, What*

About Bob?, To Die For, Pretty Woman, One Fine Day, Volcano, and *Courage Under Fire,* had acquired the project from the Barry Mendel Company. This was the same Barry Mendel who had passed on *North Wind* over six years earlier, in 1993 when he was an agent at United Talent Agency and had replied to my classified ad in *Variety.*

Ironically, I had once thought of giving *North Wind* the same title as the Willingham script, *The Last Viking,* but to me it sounded too much like *The Last of the Mohicans.* With Crichton/Bandaras' *The 13th Warrior* in production, and now *The Last Viking,* how many other Viking scripts, I wondered, were out there? Had Barry Mendel been reading Viking scripts for six years before he found one he liked? Or was this only the second one he had read? Or had he simply tossed mine aside when he left United Talent Agency—forgotten it?—lost it?—but now wished he could re-read it to compare the two? How much better, or different, was *The Last Viking* script?

During the last week of February, Jeff Kent sent me two advance copies of the March, 1999 issue of *Symbol.* My 2000-word article ran in the "Folks" section of the magazine, and was illustrated with my "sportscaster" photo.

Entitled *A Work in Progress,* Kent's piece was a very positive man-against-the-odds profile. He did a wonderful job of weaving the quirky endorsements into the story as a way to "market" myself. The Straw Hut $1 option against the $500,000 payday was mentioned at the end, and added to the story's theme: "Perhaps he will win that lottery after all."

I immediately sent *Symbol* Managing Editor Jane Gaston a huge arrangement of flowers, and sent Kent a gift certificate to a great Atlanta restaurant.

For the publicity efforts that resulted in the *Symbol* article, I had paid Jeannie Berg a total of $2096.86 for her time and expenses. To get 1000 glossy reprints of the two-page article printed front-and-back would have cost me about $700 more. I passed. While mulling over what to do next, I bought as many copies of *Symbol* as I could find ($3.99 plus tax) in local drug and grocery stores, mailing them to producers who were actively considering my scripts.

While I was searching for additional copies of the magazine, I ran across a kids' workbook about Vikings. Filled with games, ship puzzles, a sundial and Viking lore, it also contained a set of rune stones—the Viking alphabet which could also be used for fortunetelling. *North Wind* contained a very important scene in which these stones figured. After I randomly picked the "jera" (j) stone from the kit, I read my Viking fortune: "Patience and determination are essential to truly succeed in any endeavor."

What was I to do about my relationship with Terry Porter? Should I begin looking around for another agent? My original contract with him allowed me to dismiss him on 14 days' written notice. But how do you know whether your agent is gaining momentum or has peaked? His written progress reports, which I was able to get from him only after long stretches of time—not on a monthly basis as I had so frequently requested—merely stated the names of the production companies to which he had sent various scripts. I never knew the relative "weight" of any inquiry, or how "hot" it was.

In early March, I received the Spring/Summer 1999 edition of the *Hollywood Agents & Managers Directory* ($49.95 plus shipping) which listed over 1,300 agencies and over 4,500 agents and managers, and also offered mailing labels with the names of the agents, to be peeled off and stuck on envelopes. My first thought was to send out a mass-mailing inquiry to LA based agents, enclosing my synopses and a reprint of the *Symbol* article.

But then in mid-March Terry Porter called me to report that Eric Handler and his development team at DreamWorks were again interested in discussing production and distribution of

North Wind. Terry was scheduled to be in LA to attend Ted Baehr's annual entertainment awards show, and then stay on to attend the Academy Awards ceremony on Sunday, March 21, the first time the show was aired on a Sunday night. The meeting with DreamWorks was to take place at their offices on the Universal Studios lot on Thursday, March 18. The plan was that Porter would disclose Straw Hut's option agreement on *North Wind*, and then gauge DreamWorks's interest in co-production with Straw Hut.

Maybe it wasn't time to fire Porter just yet.

I loaded a big box full of scripts, Viking books, a Viking game/activity book, and copies of *Symbol* magazine and shipped them to the Beverly Garland Hotel in North Hollywood where Terry was to stay. Upon his arrival, Terry would have a war chest of "sales" materials and gifts for the DreamWorks team.

While flipping through the *Agents Directory* book as I still pondered getting a new agent, I ran across a management company which represented adult/teen actors, comedians, lyricists, martial artists, musical artists, and screenwriters. Interestingly, they listed as a specialty representation of "disabled actors." I phoned the owner, Marie Lanaras, and pitched *Wheels*.

Marie's LA based Wild Briar Talent was going through a transition, she said, from agency to production company. She was looking for an interesting script that would educate people about the disability movement, and she had a lot of talented people in mind for the film that would result. After I had done my pitch, she requested a copy of *Wheels*, which I then sent along with a copy of the award from the Charleston International Film Festival, Max Cleland's letter, and of course a *Symbol* magazine.

One evening a few days later, Marie left a message on my voicemail saying she had received *Wheels*, was enjoying it, but it was missing page 53. Would I please fax it to her home immediately! I had recently photocopied five sets of *Wheels*, and all of them were missing page 53, which did in fact contain a key scene with crucial dialogue. Perhaps the omission of the page sparked her interest all the more.

I faxed page 53 to Marie. Maybe omitting a page here and there from other scripts would be a good marketing tool for other submissions?

By March 16, Terry was winging his way to Los Angeles from Indiana. Since neither of us had heard from Joe Rowland for a long time, I sent him a casual e-mail inquiring about Marlene Mendoza's progress in selling *North Wind*, and asking if I could get a photocopy set of the storyboards for my scrapbook.

I was startled by the reply from Straw Hut. It seemed that due to their previous worries about the short length and viability of *North Wind*, the fact that there were too many "Viking" projects around, the re-write needs of the story, etc., *North Wind* was "on hold." Huh? The thrust of their reply was that the movie industry is "just about money, not about talent or scripts"—but "get back to us, or we will to you, if a co-producer or other attachments are found."

About money, indeed! What about mine?

The meeting with DreamWorks on the Thursday of Oscar Week took on even greater importance. The option by Straw Hut would end on June 16, 1999, unless Joe Rowland paid me another dollar for an additional six months. Would DreamWorks want to co-produce *North Wind* sooner with Straw Hut, or grab the script for themselves once the option period lapsed at a later date?

Upon arriving home on the night of the Scathing E-Mail From Straw Hut, I found a message waiting from Marie Lanaras of Wild Briar, the lady with the missing page 53, saying she wanted to buy an option on *Wheels* for the "same deal as your other current option." I called her, we chatted a few minutes, and I offered to track down Terry Porter and have him give her a call, or perhaps a visit, while he was in LA during the week. Perhaps, I suggested to her, Terry knew other interested parties who could come together, and pool their resources. I ended by saying that I "had to get my agent's final recommendation" before committing to anything.

Marie had no production or directing experience, but the passion in her voice told me that she was on a mission. Marie wasn't "only about money." Her mission was to demonstrate to the uninitiated that talented, disabled, wheelchair-enabled actors were in abundance and being overlooked by Hollywood. *Wheels* would provide the means to prove her point, and to start her on a movie production career path that was paved with her knowledge of talent.

When men and women make a point of claiming they have no experience in something, yet make no apologies because they know their raw talent, courage, and endurance will overcome any obstacle ... well, that kind of stuff inspires most of us. Marie inspired me.

Chapter 12

Into the Briar Patch

The day after the Oscars, Monday, March 22, 1999, Ted Baehr called me at home at 10 p.m. to request that I overnight a copy of *North Wind* to him the following day, so that he could send it to Mel Gibson's company at Paramount. Mel's company had asked Dr. Ted about historical scripts, and Ted immediately suggested *North Wind*. I sent Ted a script, a synopsis, more copies of the *Symbol* magazine that featured Ted's quote, and another Viking activity game/book set as a gift for ... er, uh, well ... Mel.

Earlier in the day, Marie Lanaras called to ask if I had heard from Terry Porter over the previous few days, and I told her that I had not. Terry should have been on his way to meet with her to discuss the option for *Wheels*, and, apparently lost in LA, he had not surfaced! He still might have been circling the freeway looking for an off-ramp for all she knew ...

Still earlier that day, Straw Hut sent me a final e-mail stating their absolute non-interest in pursuing *North Wind* further, yet they didn't offer to immediately cancel their option. If they had, I was going return their uncashed check, frame and all.

While I was waiting for Terry and Marie to complete their negotiations on the *Wheels* option and present it to me, Marie requested an original copy of the script from which she could make multiple photocopies any time she wished. I sent her two originals, a 114-page version and a 121-page version. While they were exactly the same script, by setting the page margins differently, numbering each scene on the pages, and using other tweaks, I increased the length of the script by seven pages. This way, I gave her a choice: 120 pages for those people who insisted on having one minute of action for every page of a two-hour movie, or a shorter version for those who thought less is more, because that left room for creative input later.

In another e-mail, Marie mentioned that she had once lived in Georgia, and now in Los Angeles, occasionally missed "real" Southern cooking. As an act of goodwill, I promptly sent her a Redneck Survival Kit of grits, country gravy mix, corn bread mix, and package of beef jerky. I try to take care of the people around me, and spare no expense. The grocery bill was $5.07 plus tax. She loved the package.

The first draft of Marie's option agreement arrived in mid-April under her maiden name Terre Worhach. Her full maiden name was Theresa Marie Worhach, and after divorcing a Mr. Lanaras, she had decided to go back to her maiden name with Theresa abbreviated. She also decided to make a name transition from the talent agency to her production company, moving from Wild Briar Talent to Briar Patch Productions.

✳✳✳

In mid-April, Terry Porter alerted me that Mel Gibson was personally reading *North Wind*. He also confirmed that he and Ted Baehr had made it known to DreamWorks and Mel Gibson's company at Paramount that the other was "actively reviewing" the script, hoping to spur collaboration or even a bidding war.

The folks at Kinkos were as delighted as I was, saying that they would not use the machine on which Mel's copy had been photocopied until the script was purchased. An inspirational gesture on their part, a good story to tell, but figured they were just carried away by the moment. They did, however, give me a corporate discount on photocopies, either as a reward or because they felt sorry for me. I'm sure I had paid for the photocopy machine all by myself.

It was at this time that I also found an e-mail pen pal on the Internet. I had posted an e-mail message on the web site of the visitors' bureau of the city of Durham, England, looking for Viking artifacts, toys, games, and replicas to use as future gifts as I continued to market *North Wind*. I received a reply from Jennie Walker, originally from Durham but then living in York, who told me of the internationally famous Viking educational amusement park Jorvik Centre there, which I had already known about. She wrote of the annual Viking festival which included actual boat burnings on the River Ouse. (No mention of people alive or dead in the boats at the time.) This was also the land of the important Roman city of Eboracum, Jennie reported. She lived in York with her small child and her husband, a regional journalist and wannabe novelist. The Internet was making the world a very small e-place.

York was also a place of conquest by Mel Gibson's William Wallace in *Braveheart*, a fact I remembered while watching the video, after receiving Jennie's e-mail.

One other e-mail pen pal who surfaced from the Durham web site was Catherine Payne. Like Jennie Walker, Catherine had lived in the heart of British Viking territory, but she was in Canada at the time we corresponded. Catherine requested a copy of *North Wind* and promptly responded with an e-mail stating that while she loved the story, the script contained several historical inaccuracies and inconsistencies. A student of history, she supplied a list of books to consult when the movie rolled into production. I was grateful for the feedback, and appreciated even more the prospect of having an historical consultant for props, costuming, and the like when the rewriting process would begin.

But I just couldn't sit still and wait. I purchased three gift memberships to The Viking Heritage society at Gotland University in the names of Mel Gibson, Steven Spielberg, and DreamWorks producer Eric Handler at a total cost of US $69. I gave instructions that the membership materials, including books and newsletters, be sent to my home address. My plan was to give them to Terry Porter and Ted Baehr to send on to Mel Gibson and the DreamWorks guys as yet more gifts. From a marketing perspective, this exemplified the principle of "frequency of message"—that is, bombarding the "prospect" with multiple "sales messages."

Dr. Baehr saw merit in my "gift program," and asked for additional Viking books as well as a Viking Heritage Society membership for Cindy Bond, producer of *The Joyriders*, who claimed Viking descent and was the partner of Norm Miller of NorAnn Entertainment. I had just finished reading Norm Miller's inspirational autobiography *Beyond the Norm* about his rise to Chairman of Interstate Batteries. So, I had the Viking Heritage Society send gift memberships in my name and Dr. Baehr's name to Bond and Norm and his wife Anne. NorAnn was sought by Dr. Ted as an additional source of funding.

✳✳✳

Terre Worhach's (aka Marie Lanaras) boyfriend Biff Yeager also loved *Wheels*, and pledged to help her find talent, financing and distribution through his own contacts. At the time, he had played bit parts in over 250 movies (*Edward Scissorhands, Another 48 Hours, Sid and Nancy, Ed Wood, Batman Returns*), TV shows, and commercials.

Biff was trying to produce some screenplays of his own. His web site featured a rundown of his projects and an invitation to invest. Under his Silver Penny Productions banner, the home page of the web site announced: "Warning!!! The following is not for the feint (sic) of heart." What followed was a list of rewards for investing: at the low end, for $10, a dated, autographed picture of

Biff. At the high end, for $100,000, the same autograph, plus a T-shirt boasting *I helped finance a Major Motion Picture with Biff Yeager*, an autographed copy of the script, an 8-minute highlight video of Biff's movie career, the backer's name to grace a 'thank-you' ad in *Variety*, screen credit as Co-Executive Producer, and a trip to the premiere of the film by way of a personal limousine service. Here was someone even wackier and more desperate than I was (in a good way)!

Both the gift memberships to the Viking Heritage Society for Spielberg, Gibson, and Handler, and my contract from Terre Worhach, arrived on April 26, 1999. The back-and-forth between Terry and Terre produced a one-year option agreement for *Wheels* that contained the following:

- For compensation for *Wheels,* I would receive the greater sum of the Writers Guild Minimum (at that time $62,571) or 3% of the entire production budget. Rewrites would be negotiated separately, but the WGA minimum was then $22,758 per rewrite. Payment would be at the end of production but before release to the theatres.
- The Christopher Reeve Foundation, United States Paralympics, and Momentum International would equally share a percentage of the overall compensation, including future television residuals.
- For the one-year option, I would receive $1.

Another buck. The $1 check from Terre came. At least the checks were now coming from Hollywood, even if the amount was insignificant, although wife Darrah reminded me that the priority was the reverse.

I quickly signed the option contract and sent it back to Terre. I countersigned another copy for Porter, and mailed it out with another dime for his 10% commission, and included the Spielberg and Handler Viking Membership packets for him to forward. Spielberg and Handler became Viking Heritage member numbers 386 and 385, respectively.

I sent the Gibson packet to Baehr. Mel was member number 387.

In mid-May, I learned that the editor who had written my article for *Symbol Magazine*, Jeff Kent, had lost his job when his magazine was purchased by the cross-town competitor *Atlanta Magazine*, which promptly shut down *Symbol*. Having by then been downsized five times myself, I offered Jeff my heartfelt condolences.

In a letter dated May 14, Terre received her first rejection for *Wheels* from Helen Hunt's company, Hunt/Tavel Productions. Creative Executive Jason D. Scott wrote that the script wasn't "funny" enough. Ouch! The letter ended with the encouragement to Terre from Scott to "keep plugging away ... your spirit and patience should guide you well."

✳✳✳

I had found Terre/Marie Worhach/Lanaras in the *1999 Hollywood Agents & Managers Directory*, which also had but a single listing for a Writers Guild registered agency based in Atlanta where I was living. WriterStore was a subsidiary of the nationally recognized talent agency The People Store. WriterStore was run by Rebecca Shrager and Brenda Eanes. I sent an e-mail solicitation and a copy of the *Symbol* article to Brenda, who in reply requested *Wheels*, *CATV*, and *Cleaning Up*.

I explained to Brenda my history of options, agents, and the current promising status of Porter and Baehr's effort to sell *North Wind*. WriterStore had opened its business in the fall of 1998 and had but a few writers at that point, but in fact its goal was to take on only about a half dozen or so screenwriters. After reading "hundreds and hundreds" of scripts they had decided to sign very few of their authors to contracts, they claimed.

By late May, Brenda indicated that she wanted to represent

me. She said that I wrote great dialogue. By that time, I had been with Terry Porter for almost three years, and a clause in our contract allowed me to cancel with just 14 days' notice. According to the Writers Guild, Porter would then have 12 months to sell those scripts he had pursued, namely *Wheels, Scattered Seeds,* and *North Wind.*

What to do? Sign with WriterStore, a hot start-up agency with existing contacts in the business and a client list so small I would be guaranteed lots of personal attention? WriterStore would try to sell all seven of my scripts, not just two or three as had Porter, or even Hopkins or Glass before him. Maybe an Atlanta agency representing an Atlanta writer would mean something—or nothing? Or should I just bide my time and send out a lot of query letters, hoping for an LA-based agency? What about my loyalty to Terry Porter? What would a move now do to his motivation to close a deal for *North Wind* since we were seemingly getting closer to a sale?

Maybe I was over-thinking the problem. Maybe I wasn't thinking hard enough.

I decided to sign with WriterStore. Even though they had no sales as an agency at that point, they had convinced me that they had no problem getting the attention of any studio in Hollywood. One of my calls to Brenda interrupted, she said, a call from Robin Williams' agent, and I believed her. She had no reason to try to impress me; quite the opposite was true. I sent an e-mail to Porter and then on May 22, 1999, followed-up with a registered letter. Porter would have until May 20, 2000, to sell *North Wind, Wheels,* and *Scattered Seeds.*

✳✳✳

My sixth corporate downsizing, from Fred Mort's Fantastic Sports, Inc., came on a Thursday afternoon in June without warning and without a severance check. None. Rigor mortis. (The company, however, demanded six *weeks'* notice if employees left on their own accord!)

Mort had sold the company to an investment holding company (which in turn was sold thereafter), and it was now time to cut their expenses, cut speculative new business efforts, and let's face it, make the books look better. But patience does have its reward, and potential clients I had been courting for some months decided within days of my leaving to remain loyal to me and place their contracts with me—actually, help me start my own marketing services agency in the process. A big windfall, and a de facto severance package. Tactically, I would be creating contests, sweepstakes, and sports marketing programs, while coordinating all the legal work and printed materials to support these efforts.

To handle the workload, I incorporated The Viking Group, Inc. on July 1, 1999, the same day that Darrah and I celebrated our 10th wedding anniversary. Starting from an office at home, I caught a further glimpse of what I hoped the future would hold for a stay-at-home screenwriter. (And the company name reminded me of the importance of selling *North Wind ...* soon!)

✳✳✳

June 16, 1999, came and went without Straw Hut Entertainment continuing their option on *North Wind.* The script was now free and clear, and Terry Porter pressed for a meeting with DreamWorks.

A July 7 e-mail from Terry Porter reported that development executive Eric Handler at DreamWorks had decided "to pass" on *North Wind.* No reason given other than "upper management decision ..." No meeting. No next step. Six months of waiting and hoping, all gone.

NorAnn passed shortly thereafter.

The fact that DreamWorks had held onto *North Wind* for a total of some 18 months led us to believe that they liked the writing, but the script was killed for some other reason; too costly?—not right for a director/actor they had in mind for a project?—the development team was over-budget for the year?—the development team was leaving for another studio and wanted to take the script with them? So many possible behind-the-scenes scenarios. Would DreamWorks now consider any of my other scripts? Would DreamWorks reconsider if Mel Gibson wanted to do the film with them?

Porter committed to helping Dr. Ted press the issue with Mel Gibson and his Icon company in order to gauge any continued interest on their part.

✳✳✳

On August 31, 1999, my mind was far from focused on screenwriting. Andy, then 4, was to have his first official YMCA soccer practice for the co-ed 4/5- year-old league. His first organized sports experience outside of winning the blue ribbon for running 30 yards against other kids at a local fair. I had volunteered for the position of Assistant Coach, although football, baseball, basketball, and track had consumed my youth, and I had never played organized, or even disorganized, soccer. Soccer season overlapped with other sports that I knew how to play.

Each team was named for a country, and Andy's was Team USA.

The emotional significance of Andy's first practice swept over me like one of those waves at the beach which quietly, suddenly, and unexpectedly knock you down when you're looking the other way. Even today, that first short practice which lasted but an hour seems days in length.

On the drive to the practice field, we stopped at my mom's house to say hello. Andy wanted to show-off his new cleats, shorts, and shin guards. Dad had died the previous year, and Mom remarked that "he would still be there, watching," just as he did with my practices.

The practice started a little late because one of the girls found a nest of lady bugs next to the field and other kids had to look as well. The kids then took great joy in learning the skills—each drill was a fun game to be played. Sometimes their attention drifted, so the drills were changed frequently.

One kid called me "coach," the first time that had ever happened. It hit me in the gut, the same way I felt when Andy first called me "Daddy." It expressed a level of responsibility that was suddenly humbling. I was in charge of an athletic experience which could influence a lifetime—or not. Maybe I was heaping too much significance on the day. Maybe not.

I tried to treat Andy like all the other players. Not too much attention, not too little. He still called me Daddy, not Coach, but that was OK.

There was some envy in it for me. I wanted to have a new pair of cleats and run down the open field. A flood of memories of my own practices came to mind as the hot sun set behind the Georgia pines. I didn't think I would miss it so—more than 20 years after the last time I wore cleats. I was jealous.

The fastest sprint of the day was to the adjacent school playground after the practice had concluded. There were slides to slide and swings to swing. The cleats wouldn't do—most flung them off and went barefoot. The kids compared notes as to which they liked best—Burger King or McDonald's—meaning the toys, not the food. Who was stronger?—Batman or Superman. Was Buzz Lightyear really an alien? What's an alien? The playground was but an extension of the practice field, a seamless exploration for them of the world of imagination and play. I was jealous.

On the way to the parking lot, I took Andy's hand in mine to cross the street, and when I did, I felt my Dad's hand grasp my own.

✳✳✳

A September 14, 1999, e-mail from Terry Porter reported that Mel Gibson had decided to pass on *North Wind*.

That same night, I had the worst nightmare that a screenwriter could have: I was in a stalled office building elevator between floors with Kevin Costner, Sylvester Stallone, Michelle Pfeiffer, Julia Roberts, Kim Basinger, and Robin Williams, and when we began to chat, I completely forgot the plots to any of my screenplays. I awoke at 3:30 a.m.

Must have been something I ate.

*** * ***

October 1999 sports news: Andy's Team USA finished their season 5-1-2, with Andy scoring a key goal in the rain against Team Norway for the final win. Andy was excited to receive his first trophy—the first *soccer* trophy for a member of the Catherman family. Head Coach Jim Crawford and myself each received a bottle of wine from the parents in appreciation.

The next spring, in his second season, Andy scored 37 of his team's 43 goals in a mirror 5-1-2 season.

I attended Marist School's homecoming football game in October 1999 with classmate Tommy Smith to celebrate our 25th Year Class Reunion, with the War Eagles winning the school's 500th football game in a history dating back to 1903 (without fielding a team from 1904 to 1911 and in 1913). I played in 11 of those victories.

That same October, Terry Porter was in LA, attending a private advance screening of *Toy Story II* and pitching *Scattered Seeds*. Porter had two leads: the always-Civil-War-interested TNT Originals, and the film-making division of Harlequin Books, also looking for historical scripts.

Andy was a dinosaur for his school Halloween party, then switched to a Zorro costume on Halloween night. His cape and mask in the Licensed Products Age were more effective than my own homemade versions when I was his age.

Also in October, I bought a customized license plate for my car: MVERTR (moviewriter). It brought a smile to my face every time I got in or out of the car, no matter what mood I was in.

Terre Worhach was still aggressively pitching *Wheels* to studios, co-financing sources and anyone else who would listen.

We turned back the clocks an hour. Thus ended October. Would I ever sell a screenplay? Were my prayers getting stuck to the roof of my bedroom ceiling? Did God care if I sold a screenplay? If He gave me the gift to write, why wasn't He allowing me to achieve commercial success? What was His plan in this? Was His plan unfolding, and I just wasn't understanding?

✳✳✳

With a number of small up-and-coming producers constantly emerging, the back classified pages of *Variety* and *The Hollywood Reporter* usually listed names of film companies seeking scripts. I would send them my one page synopses of all my scripts along with my *Symbol* article, never bothering to get my agent(s) involved, and for the price of a stamp, never anticipating a response. Usually, no response was received.

However, my reply to an ad for Rebellion Pictures in New York, seeking "a script for production in Summer 2000 … (which) must be edgy, unique, and intelligent …" bore fruit when they called and requested copies of *Wheels* and *CATV*. I informed them of the current option on *Wheels*, but I also made a commitment to introduce them to Terre Worhach should they want to do a joint venture. As for *CATV*, I told them it was edgy, unique and intelligent (what else were they expecting me to say?!).

Was this the start to my first sale?

✳✳✳

On December 13, 1999, Terre Worhach told me she was giving up on *Wheels*. She just couldn't sell it with the contacts she had (or didn't have), and she didn't want to stand in my way. I appreciated her ethics and honesty. She would send a letter releasing the option on *Wheels*, which was to have run another four months, until April 15, 2000. Terry Porter was happy because he again had control of *Wheels* at the very moment that "four studios are pounding down my door looking for comedies … including Paramount Pictures!" quoth he.

On the same day, after months of little feedback from them, Brenda and Rebecca at WriterStore e-mailed to say they had just returned from a script-selling junket to LA, and while the feedback on *Cleaning Up* was very positive, "every" producer wanted "free rewrites" before they would consider purchasing the script. But they neglected to give any specific feedback about the kind of changes they wanted. This sounded like a simple brush-off from the studios, and although WriterStore urged me to start making script changes (in a vacuum with no specifics), I said, "No, thanks."

How do you begin to make changes without any feedback, anyway? Mind-reading was not my strength. If a producer (i.e., the Development Executive) wanted changes, he could buy the script first, and then either hire me or another writer to do rewrites. That's why they call it "development," right? Where would you start without having any "notes" to guide you? I set up a face to face meeting with Rebecca on December 21 to discuss these issues: it was our first meeting of this kind, even though to have such a conference was one of the reasons why I selected an Atlanta-based agency. This meeting was at the time literally right down the street from my home, no more than a mile or so.

Chapter 13

Catch-22

The *Oxford English Dictionary* defines a "Catch-22" as a circumstance that presents a dilemma because of mutually conflicting or dependent situations.

※※※

On August 5, 1999, I had a message from agent Brenda Eanes at WriterStore with some feedback she had received about *Cleaning Up* from Punch (Dustin Hoffman's company), Castle Rock, and Rastar (housed at Columbia Tristar):

1. Needs more character development
2. The romance happens too fast
3. The young lead guy does not go thru any kind of transformation
4. Everything is much too fast

She concluded by suggesting that "…I think you might want to consider a few rewrites. Let me know your thinking."

I had been through the extensive, day-in and day-out rewrite process with *Vengeance* and the guys at Trident years before. And I had done some minor rewrites with Jason Hervey on *Wheels*. I had learned the process necessary to perform a professional rewrite that reflected the very subtle nuances of the creative vision of the producer or the director. I enjoyed that collaborative process. The very *business* of screenwriting *was* rewriting, that much I did know.

There has never been and never will be a first-draft script written that is ready to shoot and that incorporates the total vision of the producer and director. Never. That's why there's something called the "development" phase. In fact, this process is often so laborious that it has earned the nickname "development hell."

But call it development or not, the first step is for the studio/producer to buy the script, or treatment, or oral pitch, or two-page outline, or novel, or magazine article—whatever the source from which a script will be written or adapted. After that, the original screenwriter, per Writers Guild rules, gets a shot at rewrites before other screenwriters can be hired to hack away. Final screenwriting credit, if not clearly defined, can be shared through an arbitration-like process involving the Writers Guild. Many times the final group of screenwriters whose names appear on the screen credits never meet. Witness *The Flintstones* movie and many others.

I wasn't going to do rewrites for free. And even if I was inclined that way, the feedback I received was much too generalized for me even to begin the procedure. The resulting script would be "different," but would it be "better?" How many free rewrites did WriterStore or the producers above wish to see before they bought the script? An infinite number?

Catch-22: do rewrites for studios before they tell you which rewrites they want.

I replied to this e-mail from Brenda the same day by citing the David Rafael book *Eyes Wide Open* in which he goes into great and wonderful detail about the rewriting process that became *Eyes Wide Shut*, Stanley Kubrick's last movie. Rafael was paid anew every step of the way, for every draft, and the script was discussed line by line with Kubrick. Plot, dialogue, setting, pacing, you name it.

Was my ability to do rewrites being tested? Was the agency's

ability to bully their writers to do free work being tested? Was a
purchase imminent, except for small changes which could be fixed
later …? There wasn't enough feedback for me to know. Since my
e-mail and subsequent phone calls were not returned, I assumed
that WriteStore at least understood my views on rewriting in a
vacuum, without adequate feedback, and rewriting for free. I simply felt they were getting the "professional" brush-off from the
studios, while simply leaving the door open in case I wanted to do
some rewrites. What did *they* have to lose?

But, on September 21, just a month later, another e-mail arrived for me from WriterStore. Without responding to the issues I
had previously raised, Brenda reported that she "liked *CATV* very
much, but didn't like the ending." She went on to say that
WriterStore would try to sell my script *if* I would agree that "should
two or three producers not like the ending," I would rewrite it!

Huh?

In a few paragraphs via return e-mail, and with three minutes
of thought, I suggested *five* different ways the ending to *CATV*
could be changed. I'm sure I could have suggested fifty, given a
day to think about it. I also suggested that the beginning and
middle could or would be changed by anyone who read the script.
It's a murder mystery, and therefore could accommodate lots of
twists and turns.

I communicated to the agent as tactfully as possible that her
opinion didn't count. She hadn't sold or developed dozens of scripts,
and as William Goldman said on behalf of screenwriters every-
where, "no one knows anything." The only opinion about future
changes that counted was the opinion of the producer who would
write the check to buy the screenplay.

My message, again, was that I wasn't going to do rewrites.
Again, no response came via e-mail or phone … until December,
when another e-mail arrived inquiring about my interest in rewriting my scripts. Now. For no money.

Huh?

What part of 'no' didn't they understand? I had an agency that was successfully getting me no-paying jobs to do rewrites with no direction. Swell. They can have 10% of that.

I finally was successful in reaching Rebecca Shrager, the agency head, on the phone and scheduled a meeting for December 21. A week before the meeting was even scheduled, I had sent Christmas gifts to Brenda and Rebecca: Warner Brothers and Disney trivia games. I didn't know what was proper etiquette, or whether it was more appropriate for the agency to send gifts to the writers, but I gave gifts to people, lots of people, almost year-round for various reasons, or no reason, because it's fun. I hoped that the gifts going before me would somehow soften any blows in the meeting to follow.

✳✳✳

What I needed was a "manager." I had just finished Bernie Brillstein's book entitled *You're No One in Hollywood Unless Someone Wants You Dead: Where Did I Go Right?* Bernie was the legendary entertainment manager who had discovered and represented Jim Henson, Lorne Michaels, John Belushi and the Saturday Night Live gang (actually riding alone in a small corporate jet beside the deceased Belushi en route to the funeral), and even produced the movie *Dangerous Liaisons* and lots of television. The book was of interest to me because of its behind-the-scenes stories of turf wars with Mike Ovitz and others in Hollywood, but more importantly because the book explained the subtle differences between the role of an entertainment *manager* versus that of an *agent.*

For example, while the manager could help round up a screenwriter, script, director, and actor and put them in a "package" to sell to a studio, it was the agent who had to negotiate the final contract terms, by law, although it appeared the manager would also field and negotiate offers. Agents had to be State licensed:

not so, managers. Managers, however, at times sought further "protective" control of the talent and script by negotiating a "producer" role for themselves. At best, the managers and agents, pooling their resources and contacts, made the best deal at the right time for the talent they jointly represented. At worst, the talent was yanked apart as the manager and agent sought to control the talent, the product, and the process. It could get ugly, fast.

My take on the situation was that a manager could act as a catalyst for an agent: using either the carrot or the stick when needed. That's what prompted me to send a query letter to 85 managers listed in the *1999 Agents and Managers Directory*. Although the screenwriter was giving away additional percentages of the script's sale price, a smaller percentage of a sale was better than no sale at all. Widening the field of prospective buyers could be achieved: I could have both an agent and a manager trying to sell my scripts, and hopefully (and wishfully), acting as teammates to urge one another onward, combining resources and contacts.

In my query letter to the 85 managers, I sent a copy of the *Symbol Magazine* article, one-sheet synopses of my scripts, a copy of the Charleston Film Festival notification of the award for *Wheels*, a copy of Max Cleland's endorsement of that script and, finally, a self-addressed stamped envelope as a courtesy.

I was anticipating the usual catch-22 from some of them: if you're not good enough for us to call you, don't call us.

✳✳✳

What was I going to wear to the WriterStore meeting on December 21? Surely not my Brooks Brothers Corporate Uniform. What did real screenwriters wear to visit their agents? I needed to wear something black. Every creative person wore black, right? I settled on a black shirt, black pants, and black shoes. Creative, yet professional. "Hollywood," yet "Southern."

I guessed that real screenwriters drove a black two-seat convertible Mercedes or BMW to their meetings. Or, these days, black

Mercedes SUVs. Or took a limo. I once had a bright, hot, red convertible Alfa Romeo Spider which Darrah bought for me for my birthday one year, and I drove around in it while pretending I was Robert Redford's Hubble Gardner in *The Way We Were*. Although I currently drove a 1997 silver Nissan Altima (and still do), it did have the MVERTR license plate. I was a screenwriter, at least for the day.

The meeting with agency head Rebecca Schrager lasted less than an hour. I rehashed my position that I was ready, willing, and able to make any and all changes that a buyer would want— without exception and without complaint—except that the script had to be purchased first. Rebecca reiterated their position that while not a perfect situation, none of my scripts would be pitched in the future unless and until I first made all of the changes that they, the agency, deemed necessary.

Huh? *Which* changes?

They represented a dozen writers by then, meaning that I was receiving less personal attention than I had been lead to believe I would, but they had not sold a single script of any writer in the year since they began repping screenwriters, according to them. I wondered why.

I posed a quick solution to which agency owner Rebecca agreed: she would read *CATV* (because only Brenda, her agent, had read it) and *Wings on High* by February 1, 2000, and if these didn't meet her creative standards "as-is," then we would dissolve our relationship immediately. She had already passed on *Brothers' Brunch* and refused to continue to send out *Cleaning Up*. If the relationship dissolved in February, which was now my objective, WriterStore wouldn't get to rep *Wheels*, *North Wind*, or *Scattered Seeds* when these came out of Porter's shop in May, the date his Agreement with me would terminate. I didn't want to have the scripts tied-up in the WriterStore shop, sitting idle because I refused to do rewrites for free based on their vision of what the stories should become, while waiting for our contractual agreement to expire in June of 2001. With Porter's agreement due to end, I could extend my agreement with him if he so chose, which I expected he would. Or, better yet, I could have an LA-based manager by then who could help me find an LA-based agent. What a chess game this was becoming.

I never heard back from WriterStore. Good news.

✳✳✳

On December 31, 1999, at the dawn of a new millennium, I received my first manager query reply from Jerry Goldstein of Goldstein Company, Inc., and at the bottom of my letter to him, a handwritten note which read:

"Save your pennies. Commit to LA for at least 18 to 24 months. Network, find an agent and a manager—chances of making 'it' from Atlanta are minuscule. Good Luck, Jerry G."

Funny, but on that day, even after that letter, I still felt more optimistic about my chances to sell a script, no matter where I was living, than at any other time. Catch-22: being optimistic in the face of continued rejection.

Chapter 14

Hanks for Nothing

In March, 2000, a few days before the Oscars, friend Jeff Kaufman spotted Tom Hanks eating alone at The Varsity restaurant in Atlanta, the best place in the world for chili dogs, and only a couple miles from my house. Jeff and I ate there for lunch from time to time. Would I have been there, I know I would have thoroughly embarrassed myself, but not before pitching a script or two. One on one. Over onion rings. Either I would have gotten arrested … or sold something.

That same week, after telling Terry Porter of the Hanks-miss, he e-mailed back saying that on one of his infrequent trips to LA he had had similar "bad luck." Wrote Porter:

"Dang. Sounds like my luck at DreamWorks last Friday. I was invited to a party and said no. It was Leonardo DiCaprio's birthday party in Santa Monica at a warehouse all catered and live Rap Bands, etc., tight security. Oh well, who would have THUNK it … ha."

Huh? Turn down a DreamWorks party? Perhaps it was lucky, I thought, that my agreement with Terry, which began in July, 1996, was coming to an end in May, 2000. He sounded tired. A little distracted. I bought the 2000 edition of the *Agents and Managers Directory* and began to send out query letters to 105 LA-based agents.

Chapter 15

Grits

The reply letters from agents and managers began to come in during the Spring of 2000. One agent said he wasn't interested in reading my material, but recommended somebody who evaluates scripts for a fee. That same day, I received a letter from another agent who replied that he wasn't interested in reading my material and couldn't even supply the name of a person who evaluates scripts for a fee, because "the Writers Guild has advised that this is against their policy." The same letter also added a P.S., reminding me that "only agents, not managers, can negotiate on your behalf." The Hatfields (agents) & McCoys (managers) meet Hollywood.

One agent, by way of apology for sending a form rejection letter, replied that he received "20 query letters a day from all over the world." Multiply that by the number of days the mail is delivered, and you get about 5,000 queries a year. If each query pitches 2 scripts (versus mine which pitched seven), that's 10,000 new scripts seeking representation and production. A lot.

✳✳✳

From time to time, I still wandered around the Internet, typing in search phrases such as "studios seeking screenplays," and "producers buying scripts," and "wanna buy a lot of great damn screenplays for cheap?" In March, the search engine landed on JustUs Productions, based in Los Angeles, which was accepting queries via e-mail. Upon e-mail query/reply, they wanted to read all seven of my scripts.

JustUs Productions was owned by Mr. Pat Finerty and Ms. Barbara Wade. Pat was hosting a successful weekly program on KWHY, *The Business Channel*. He also helped launch the Computer Cable Network in 1995 as co-host and segment producer. His background was in hosting award-winning cable television and radio productions.

Barbara's background included stints as a news anchor and stand-up comedienne. While in Atlanta, she launched cable's *Single Vision* and hosted its *What's the Point?* talk-show, touted as "the hottest show to watch with the most engaging host." She also co-hosted and produced the health-related show *Fit and Focused*, which ran for three years in several major markets.

I sent JustUs all seven scripts, and wanting to be somehow remembered a little more than all the other writers, I sent along a box of grits, knowing that Barbara probably missed this southern dish.

Barbara voicemailed later that month to say they had received "thousands" of queries and scripts, but *North Wind* had become an immediate favorite and, at least for the present time, placed "on top of the pile." I returned her call, and she restated her great interest in the Viking script (and the grits). Barbara also said she would soon have plenty of time to read and consider scripts since she would be bedridden due to impending back surgery.

In April, I sent Barbara a basket of bath products with a note which read, in part:

"The enclosed basket and contents (containing soaps, moisturizers, sponges, etc.) are an exact replica of ones found in 1756 at a Scandinavian archaeological dig site when they unearthed a buried Viking ship filled with riches, weapons, bath products, and animal and human sacrifices—ready for Valhalla! The Vikings were ruthless, warlike, sinful and haughty, but were a clean people with soft skin. All the best for a speedy recovery!"

I hoped our senses of humor matched.

Chapter 16

Divorce

June 1, 2000, was a celebration of my brother's 36th Birthday and, at the opposite end of the spectrum, a sad day as Darrah told me, in front of our minister, that she wanted to end our marriage which was a month shy of 11 years. It would be amicable, and focused on the priority of our mutual love and care for Andy, then 5 years old.

Darrah's emotional support for my writing was the reason I had begun to write again after many years of inactivity. For that, I will always be grateful. And for being the mother of our wonderful son Andy, I will always love her.

A hopeless romantic, on July 1st I sent Darrah a dozen of her favorite flowers, yellow roses. Some habits are hard to break, and we were technically married. During the 60 days during which I waited for an apartment to come available, while I was sleeping on the couch, Darrah would change her mind twice about wanting a divorce. It was nerve-wracking.

Having recovered from my sixth downsizing in Corporate America that February, I was now employed as promotion marketing division President of Access TCA Marketing Group. More of a community and a family than a "company," the people there became a solid resource and support to me in many ways during this period. (And, everyone pledged to be on the look-out for a movie producer in their local grocery store.)

I moved out of the house and into an apartment in August, with no clear resolution on the future of our marriage. On the days I didn't have Andy stay at my house, I watched videos of him. I missed him terribly.

Chapter 17

From the Soul

In January, 2000 I entered *Wheels* in the "Screenwriting from the Soul Script Competition," sponsored by The American Screenwriters Association. The contest was "dedicated to finding the most heartwarming, soulful story of the year ... that tells a strong, character-driven story and truly has an impact on people."

Sounded like *Wheels* to me.

The Grand Prize included a trip to LA to meet with agents, managers, and legal representatives, including a session with the Director of Development from Penny Marshall's Parkway Productions, and another with Codikow Films. Finalists received trade publicity and were asked to participate as a judge for the following year's competition.

In June, I was advised that *Wheels* had advanced to the quarterfinal round. A one-page handwritten critique generally gave the script high marks for structure, originality, plot, characterization, dialogue, style, format, and use of visuals. However, Judge #01 noted that "it would be hard to buy into the (premise) that (the main character) could be sentenced to a wheelchair."

I replied in a letter that a year after I had written *Wheels*, a Dade City, Florida, Circuit Judge named Lynn Tepper had sentenced a youth to spend two days in a wheelchair for shooting

another youth, who as a result had to spend months in a wheelchair during recovery. I enclosed the newspaper clipping.

Whether that letter helped me or not, I was notified in July
that *Wheels* had advanced to the final round.

✳✳✳

My friend Terry Cunningham alerted me to a screenwriting
contest being held by *Entertainment Weekly* magazine. I logged on
and sent in a synopsis of *Wheels*. The contest was open to the first
1000 entries. Three winning synopses would be published in a
future *EW* issue.

✳✳✳

An article in the September 12, 2000, issue of *Business 2.0* got
my attention. It was about the ways in which Internet-based screenplay buying-and-selling was about to revolutionize the way in
which unknowns were found. Charles Slocum, director of strategic planning at the Writer's Guild, noted that of the 40,000 new
scripts registered each year, the top 10 Hollywood studios purchased only 260 "scripts on spec" (i.e., written speculatively without any guarantee of compensation) in 1999. Long odds.

Many dotcoms were profiled. Maybe they were a means of
drawing attention to the better scripts that were being overlooked
by an inefficient buying system. I decided to sign-up with
ScriptShark, a dotcom that listed some recent sales they helped
facilitate by putting buyers and sellers together—one by writer
Michael Valle entitled *Sherlock Holmes and the Vengeance of Dracula*,
which was purchased by Columbia Pictures for $1 million.

For $100 per script, ScriptShark provided a "coverage report"
(a synopsis and critique) and placed a script into one of three
categories:

> *Pass.* A nice way to say "stay with your day job"; one assumes
> you could still impress people at cocktail parties by saying
> that you were "talking to some people in Hollywood …"

Consider. An abbreviated form of coverage would be posted on their web site to be viewed by "hundreds of industry buyers who use our affiliated services on a daily basis." Hundreds? Really?

Recommend. ScriptShark helps facilitate direct submission to studios and production companies, as well as "setting you up with an agent."

For a total of $300, or $100 for each of three screenplay coverage reports, I sent *Wheels, North Wind,* and *Scattered Seeds.* I was swimming with the sharks again, hoping to be friend versus food.

The shark got me. Within a week, my two-page written evaluations from ScriptShark arrived in the mail, one each for *North Wind* and *Scattered Seeds.* Both received a "Pass." While the coverage presented a generally balanced and fair critique, any and all negative issues posed could, I felt, be fixed in the rewrite stage with the help of the producers who bought the script because they recognized its potential. The reality was that the coverage I had bought from ScriptShark both reinforced and contradicted other feedback - some paid for, some free - that I had been receiving for years. Practically, of no use.

✳✳✳

September 18 was a day which epitomized the subjective nature of the business. Two letters in the mailbox that night, along with the monthly issue of *Script* magazine. The first letter, from the American Screenwriters Association, offered congratulations for the 5th place finish that *Wheels* had garnered in their competition, which I had entered the previous January. I later learned that they had received more than 200 entries. A certificate suitable for framing was enclosed. The second missive was another two-page coverage letter from ScriptShark, this time for *Wheels,* ending in a "Pass" from them. The $300 for my three scripts had been gobbled up like chum.

Earlier in the day, I had received a request to send *Wheels* to Greg Carlson of IN8 Entertainment, whom I had queried in response to his web site posting; Greg faxed a release which I signed and returned with copies of the notifications from the Charleston International Film Festival and the American Screenwriters Association, both of which had awarded *Wheels* a Finalist nod. I also enclosed the letter from Max Cleland and the bio from *Symbol*.

Subjective business, for sure.

As I sank into my La-Z-Boy chair that evening to contemplate my next move, an advertisement in *Script* caught my attention: www.scriptpimp.com (no kidding). P.I.M.P. stood for Pipeline Into Motion Pictures. Unlike a mere Internet listing and matching service, they charged $40 per script for a simple "yes" or "no" evaluation: if yes, they would represent the script for a 5% commission. They also gave the screenwriter the option of sending $100 per script for a full evaluation and a "yes" or "no" verdict. I sent forty bucks and *Wheels*.

***

Months after my last 105 query letters to agents and managers, I had received only 25 agent responses, five of which expressed an interest in reading one or more of my scripts. One agent responded with an offer to help me rewrite *Wheels* for $1.50 per page, an unethical scam of gargantuan proportions; I reported them to the Writers Guild for punishment.

Of the 85 manager queries sent out during the previous months, only 13 came back, and of those, only five wanted to read one or more scripts. In most cases, nine months later, I was still waiting for a reply from those who still were reading my stuff. The size of the pile of scripts they had to read staggered my imagination. With the commonly spoken and unspoken rule of "don't call us, we'll call you, and if you call and bother us, it will count against you," patience remained the order of the day.

Too bad I'm not a patient person.

Chapter 18

I Shook Hands
with Pat Boone

I was invited to a fund raiser in Atlanta on October 19, 2000, for Dr. Ted Baehr and the Christian Film & Television Commission. Around two hundred guests enjoyed the evening at Dean Gardens Estate, a 32,000-square foot mansion on 60 acres of land along the Chattahoochee River, complete with its own 18-hole, par 72 golf course. My memories danced back to a similarly large house, also on the River, which belonged to Sandra Glass. My friend Terry Cunningham, by this time relocated from Atlanta to Bozeman, Montana was, interestingly, an in-law of the Dean family.

The guest of honor for the evening was Pat Boone, wearing his trademark white shoes. I approached him as he was speaking with a group of people about his ancestry which traced back to frontiersman Daniel Boone (true). I shook his hand and inquired about his daughter Debbie, and then mumbled something about enjoying his recent "heavy metal" album.

After a tour of the grounds, and some inspirational Christian music by a mother and daughter duet, Boone shared with us his 50-year perspective on the entertainment industry, and the reasons Dr. Ted's mission to educate Hollywood on the impact of entertainment on youth was so important. Dr. Ted followed with reports about some compelling research on the global effect of entertainment manufactured here in America.

Susan Wales, spouse of movie producer Ken Wales, was in attendance, and was asking for special donations or ideas to help with the Commission's awards show. Because I didn't get to speak with her before the night ended, I later sent her a letter suggesting that the Commission initiate a screenwriting competition—both to raise money as well as to tangibly demonstrate to Hollywood the kind of scripts which the Commission believed should be made. My own interest was not to help administer the contest, but to enter and, hopefully, win: after all, I already had won Dr. Ted's endorsement for *North Wind*.

Pat Boone didn't sing that evening, although I wished he had.

***

Item in the October 16, 2000 issue of *The Hollywood Reporter*: "American Producer in Rome seeks script for immediate production. Must have a great female lead role for English-speaking European actress similar to Julia Roberts. Prefer contemporary romantic comedy but open to all; any location possible."

I sent *Wheels* to Payola (true name, I'm not making this up) Bonelli at Skylark Productions, at their Rome office. If nothing else, I thought, my rejection mail would begin to include interesting stamps of the world.

Never heard back from them. No stamps.

***

On October 24, I was called for jury duty, and reported to the courthouse in downtown Atlanta. While other jury members were being tampered with (so to speak) elsewhere in the building, I settled into an overstuffed chair at taxpayer's expense ($25 for the day) and read *The First Time I Got Paid for It*, a collection of short essays written by 54 (or 55 if you count the foreword by William Goldman) of Hollywood's best screenwriters. They chronicled their very first (usually funny) experiences as a paid writer, whether of obituaries, telephone sex scripts, or something else on paper. The themes of luck, pluck, and love of storytelling ran through the herd of them. In the end, the book left me with an overwhelming feeling of optimism, and a proud sense that I belonged to a community of people (paid or unpaid) dedicated to telling a story, which could be traced back to ancient Greece (although for all their contributions to civilization, the Greeks weren't smart enough to lock in a payment plan for residuals).

I never was called to serve on a jury that day, but it was most rewarding anyway. Thanks, Fulton County.

***

The next day, October 25, wasn't as much fun. In the morning, I was informed by the Access Promotions Board of Directors that my tenure as President was ending after only a couple months on the job, having transferred down the hall from its sister division, M-squared Creative. They didn't think I could turn the company around (it was still bleeding badly), although they never had tried any of my creative revenue-generating approaches to acquiring and retaining customers. For me, it was two months of business-as-usual under their system, although I did manage to bring in some revenue during that time. What made it worse was that I had to split my time between the two sister divisions, diverting my attention from both. The company didn't understand promotional marketing, what it took to differentiate themselves from the hoards of other similar businesses; they didn't want to learn it; and they certainly didn't want to plow more money into it after a couple years of trying before I came along. They now wanted to get out of promotional marketing and cut their losses, and so they closed that business altogether to concentrate on their core strengths of trade show booth construction and corporate hospitality—things they were great and very profitable at doing, but things I knew nothing about.

It was the smart thing for them to do, and I certainly would miss the talented people there, especially co-owner Bruce Morrow, a one-time seminary student. The compassion and empathy he extended to me during my separation and divorce will always be remembered and appreciated. He would have made a wonderful Episcopal priest.

This was my 7th downsizing. The good news was that the clients who needed the kind of strategic and tactical thinking I could bring to the task were quick to say that they wanted me to continue to execute their promotions on a freelance basis. My Viking Group, Inc. freelance at-home promotion agency suddenly set sail again, and I had hopes for some near-term income, which eventually translated into more money than I was making at Access Promotions. I was even hired for a project by Bruce Morrow a few months after leaving his side of the sister companies.

In an era of "golden parachutes" for executives, stock options, and Internet megazillionaires, my severance package was exactly $00.00, the same as at my last downsizing.

While I sure would miss my private executive bathroom, now that I was going to work from home, I had another one waiting for me. Small irony here in that I had just completed the development and execution of an NFL football Internet marketing promotion for the headhunting web site Monster.com—which was to continue to be a daily destination for me, but for different reasons now.

Upon arriving home that same evening of the company closure, I had three voicemail messages. The first, from my brother, offering to buy me dinner. The second, from pal Terry Cunningham, pledging prayers and joint marketing projects with his own agency, Cottonwood Enterprises. And the third, from Darrah, saying that after having been separated for four months, and after waffling a few times, she had finally decided to proceed with the divorce. She would call me later.

Before I left home in August to move into my own apartment, Darrah and I had agreed on the terms of an uncontested settlement. So there was little left to do but find an inexpensive lawyer in the Yellow Pages to write it up. Darrah and I spoke before the night was over, when she returned home from an outing, and we pledged to do whatever we could to make Andy's life as special and stable as possible. I volunteered to find the lawyer and manage the paperwork flow.

It wasn't a good day. But the heart cannot reason, and for reasons beyond my comprehension, I still felt a burning optimism deep inside. I was still running, maybe limping a little, but moving forward nonetheless.

✳✳✳

Script P.I.M.P. sent a letter back with a "pass" for Wheels. Their critique was essentially a list of questions I could have answered in a rewrite. Very frustrating, mostly because their line of questions would have led me in a direction that would have stamped their vision on the story—not better than anyone else's, just different. I paid $40 to find out I had not guessed correctly about how they would conceive the picture. I don't have a crystal ball big enough to tell me where someone wants a story to go.

I could have, and would have, made any changes they wanted if I had thought they mirrored the changes a paying producer wanted.

✳✳✳

Job hunting. Just to get back on the horse, writing resumes and interviewing, I answered a newspaper ad for a "sales and marketing" position with a video dating service. I was called for an interview which ended as soon as I learned the hours were generally from noon until 9 p.m., when most of the prospects showed up. The job was all sales, and no strategic or tactical marketing. Before leaving, I told the manager of my interest in exploring the service as a personal client, given my impending divorce. She gladly put me with a salesperson.

As I walked down the hallway to her office, I noticed pictures of happy couples along the walls—all ostensibly happily "matched" customers. The saleswoman boasted of her matchmaking prowess, which produced not only marriages but also her "other grandchildren."

It cost thousands of dollars to buy an annual or longer-term membership that entitled the member to browse the library of photos, biographies, and video interviews (in-person or online). The staff then coordinated the match-ups, giving out names and phone numbers when both parties agreed to get together. When the saleswoman went for the close, I told her I'd be willing to pay a very, very small fraction (naming the dollar amount) of the cost of the 15-month service, and without hesitation, she went to inquire of her sales manager. Upon returning, she said that her boss Okayed the amount I had offered because this was a special deal— I had been a job interviewee that day—and with the proviso that under penalty of death, or worse, I was not to tell any other member of my low introductory rate. My lucky day.

Scenes from those old western movies with the mail-order brides transported via stagecoach danced through my head. I could almost hear the wagon wheels turning and see the dust flying as the horses were halted beside the awaiting cowboy-groom, who held wilting flowers, smiling, nervous, hoping for the best.

I whipped out a credit card, and suddenly, I was in the dating game again. I couldn't afford it, at any price, but as the sales lady said, "For your happiness, you can't afford not to!" I rationalized: I did have paying freelance projects underway, my car was almost paid-off, some good job interviews loomed, and I could blow the cost of the whole membership on one bad blind date. So finding quality dates at this price suddenly seemed like a good deal.

Before leaving, I was shown some of the 1500 photos and biographical sheets of the female members (or were they just hired models?), and sure enough, it was packed with professionals just like me—women dentists, doctors, teachers, stockbrokers, and lawyers—all with too little time to find the boyfriend of their dreams. Given a *90-page* booklet to help me prepare my written biographical form and a two-minute video, I headed out to my horse in the parking lot with a mail-order-suitor-nervous smile on my face.

It occurred to me upon driving away that my life now had three very high rejection-driven parts: selling a screenplay, finding a job, and dating. Ever the optimist, I reminded myself that I needed but one success in each category.

✳✳✳

Entertainment Weekly magazine didn't pick my *Wheels* synopsis as a contest winner for its November, 2000 issue.

✳✳✳

Killing some time in a book store while waiting for a movie to start at the local mall, I ran across a book entitled *Writer's Guide to Hollywood Producers, Directors and Screenwriter's Agents* by Skip Press. Instantly I could tell the book was valuable - well researched and organized, with the producers listing their interests in terms of budget range and genre, and including fax numbers and e-mail addresses. I set about pounding away at my computer, vaulting into cyberspace with my varied synopses. My first response came within hours from producer Adam Kline (*Heaven and Earth, Reasonable Doubt, Dear Rosie*), wanting to read *Wheels* and *CATV*.

A reply to a fax sent to Beyond Entertainment came in the form of a phone call. Mr. Jun Kim, a development assistant, called at 8 p.m. Eastern time to request a copy of *Wheels*. Andy was closest to the phone, and thinking it was Darrah calling to say good night, grabbed it first. I then made some nervous, stupid remark about Andy being my assistant, and promised to send a copy of the script immediately. Kim apologized for the lateness of the call, and of course I told him to call anytime, day or night.

A real call. From Hollywood. From a real producer. Was this finally the beginning of my first sale?

Chapter 19

Matchmaking

The day before I was scheduled to do my videotaped interview at the dating service, I got a haircut. Afraid it would look like I just got a haircut, I told my stylist Rudy to just give me a "shaping." I didn't know what that meant in the parlance of haircutting, but I had heard the term around the salon. In thinking back on it, *she* wouldn't know whether I just got a haircut or not, never having seen me.

Fortunately, that morning, I didn't cut myself shaving. The shoot was at 4:30 p.m., though, so I worried about stubble. Should I take … some of my mom's makeup? How would I apply it? It being November, I didn't have a tan to cover up a lot of blotches, and I didn't have the time or interest to learn about tanning salons, so my face was going to have to go as it was.

I finished my written Profile. Under the section entitled "What I Like to Do," I listed "building sand castles on the beach, going to movies, hiking in Montana with friends, coaching youth sports, going to concerts and events like *The Nutcracker Ballet* and *Cirque du Soleil,* exercise," and finally, "enjoying things I've never done before."

Under the section entitled "Who I Am," I wrote:

"Businessman who has written award-winning screenplays and wishes to write movies for a living someday. Friends describe me as confident, safe, creative, passionate, funny, empathetic, loving, considerate, loyal, energetic, balanced, sincere, athletic, patient, joyful, industrious, spiritual, hopeful, trusting, and happy."

Did everyone lie like this?

Under the headings "Drink?" I wrote "socially." Under "Do you wish to have children?" I wrote "maybe." I assumed they meant a future child, and not Andy.

Then I faced the dilemma of what to wear. There would be four photos taken, to be arrayed on a single page—two in "semi-dress attire" and two "casual." The tips booklet told us not to look like we were going on job interviews, but if in doubt, not to dress too casually. No jeans. No T-shirts. Casual, but not. Dressy, elegant, but not too formal and stiff. "Watch out for conflicting stripes" was another warning.

Huh?

I opted for a Standard Uniform Brooks Brothers ensemble of a black sweater shirt, black pants, and a brown camel hair blazer for the formal shots, and decided I would simply take off the blazer for the "casual shots."

***

First phone call from a girl:

HER: Hi! This is (name).
ME: (nervous) Is this the tall dentist or the midget circus
    performer?
HER: (laughing) I liked your video. Are you always this funny?
ME: Just when scared to death.
HER: (laughing more)

Long pause. Silence. Beat. Beat. Beat. Beat. Sweating.

ME: So ... do you know anyone in Hollywood?

***

One entry in the *1999-2000 Writer's Guide to Hollywood Producers, Directors and Screenwriter's Agents* listed Census Film Productions, lead by Jon Scheving Thorsteinsson and Jon Einars Gustafsson. The company was based in Iceland and listed as its credits some short films, documentaries, music videos, and commercials. Gustafsson grew up in Iceland, earned his BFA in Manchester, England, and then attended the California Institute of the Arts in Valencia, California.

Were these guys descendants of real Vikings? I e-mailed them synopses of my scripts.

I received an e-mail reply from Gustafsson in early December - fittingly, a cold day in Georgia. He had moved to a warmer climate, Canada, though he was in fact a descendant of Viking settlers and an aficionado of original texts in the Viking language. He wished to read *North Wind* and *Wheels*. Since I had been turned down by DreamWorks for *North Wind*, I had been receiving Steven Spielberg's membership copies of Viking Heritage magazine, and included a couple of back issues in my package to Gustafsson.

✳✳✳

The Internet. Surfing, surfing, surfing. Playing with different combinations of words in the search engine to hopefully find an independent producer accepting screenplay submissions.

In January, 2001, at the start of yet another millennium, I traded e-mails with Jonathan Treisman of Flatiron Films. Treisman had optioned Ryan Hyde's then-unpublished manuscript *Pay It Forward*, and later served as executive producer of the movie, which starred Kevin Spacey and Helen Hunt. He was also named as one of *Variety's* "50 Creatives to Watch" in 2000, which made him 'hot,' as they say.

When Treisman informed me he was looking for comedies, I immediately sent him *Wheels*. In his friendly reply he observed that *Wheels* had "an interesting premise, however, a whole cast in wheelchairs would be a difficult sell as a major studio feature film."

I then e-queried whether *Cleaning Up* would be of interest. He quickly replied that he would like to read it. His rejection came even quicker, with a response that "Hollywood type stories (about agents and the entertainment business) are tough to sell as major feature films ..." (But are successful when made, right?)

Pass. Pass.

✳✳✳

More e-surfing. Another lead. Thura Film had headquarters in Copenhagen and offices in London and Los Angeles. Perfect, I thought, for a pitch of *North Wind*, since it takes place historically in two of their three locations. Established in 1991, Thura Film is owned by producer Michael Obel. Its international theatrical and television productions include *Nattevagten* which was directed by Ole Bomedal. The American version, *Nightwatch*, produced by Miramax and also directed by Ole Bomedal, starred Nick Nolte, Ewan McGregor, and Patricia Arquette. Its very successful run in Denmark sold 600,000 tickets, reaching more than a tenth of the country's population.

I sent an e-mail query to Lena Geert Jorgensen (a direct descendant of my main character in *North Wind*, I fantasized), and she replied quickly, requesting synopses of all seven of my scripts. There was no follow-up, no request for a copy of any of the full-length versions—just rejections shortly thereafter.

✳✳✳

I thought I would try Paulist Productions again, having recently read *Hollywood Priest*, the autobiography of its late founder, Father Bud Kieser. In response to my query, the head of development, Terry Sweeny, requested not the full-length version of *North Wind*, but rather a detailed record of where the script had been submitted. Smart question, I thought.

My detailed two-page reply recounted the activity of recent years—in other words, the rejections, by DreamWorks, Icon, and all the small independents Terry Porter had contacted without success.

On Valentine's Day, I called Sweeny to hear his verdict: pass.

He liked the premise, but wasn't interested in reading the script because he felt it might be *"overexposed!"*

Huh?

Though he had contacted no one to verify this hunch, he suggested that the Hollywood community was a small one - small enough for people to talk about rejected projects - and his organization shouldn't try to pitch the script even to those major studios that had never read *North Wind*. His efforts would be "a waste of time" for they were sure to conclude in more rejections because of the bad word-of-mouth about *North Wind*.

Overexposed?! Huh?

Sweeny did say, however, that if another producer showed interest in the script, he would be amenable to helping with co-production. So, the script is bad unless someone else wants to co-produce it? What?

✳✳✳

When Andy stayed at my house, we had a nightly ritual of storytelling and reading from a book of children's Bible stories. Andy, age 6, during the story of Adam and Eve:

> DAD: … and so, Adam ate the apple from the tree.
> ANDY: The tree that George Washington chopped down?
> DAD: No. Different tree.
> ANDY: Did Adam see her boobies?
> DAD: Yes, I guess. They didn't have clothes …
> ANDY: What kind of snake was it?
> DAD: A serpent.
> ANDY: Like a rattlesnake? Python? Cobra?
> DAD: Something like that. But the point of the story …
> ANDY: Where was the potty in the Garden?
> DAD: They went in the bushes.
> ANDY: This book is too long. Can we rent the video instead?
> DAD: (hugging my boy) Time for bed, pal. I love ya.

And on another night, this:

ANDY: ... and then God created Adam and Even, right, Dad?
ME: Who's 'Even?'
ANDY: The girl.
ME: Why did He call her 'Even?'
ANDY: Maybe 'cause she was always trying to get 'even!'

✱✱✱

Surfing. Networking. Surfing. I found Father Eddie Siebert, SJ, of Loyola Productions in Los Angeles, a Jesuit film producer. He requested a copy of *North Wind* in early February, 2001.

Fr. Eddie had started his film company in the fall of 2000, and he was searching for material to fill the pipeline. The impressive management team and advisory board included James L. Honore, Executive Vice President of Post Production for Columbia Tristar Pictures.

Fr. Eddie had served as creative consultant and technical advisor on the critically acclaimed 20th Century Fox/ABC series *Nothing Sacred*, which won a 1997 Peabody Award for excellence in broadcasting. In addition to producing, writing, and directing shorts and documentaries, his experience extended to consulting on feature films for major studios. Having completed an MFA in film production from Loyola Marymount University in Los Angeles, he had once been a member of the staff of the Sundance Film Festival.

February 26, 2001. Eight-forty five p.m. when Fr. Eddie Siebert calls to say that Loyola Productions "wants to produce *North Wind.*" The management team is excited about the script, and will now go about the job of making the rounds of their financial contacts here and in Europe. The size of the production, estimated in the tens of millions of dollars, "doesn't scare us ...," says Fr. Eddie.

I called my mom with the news, and her reaction was a mixture of joy and understatement. "Sure, I knew it would happen," she exclaimed, "because you told me to pray about Father Eddie and I did!"

Needless to say, a few more sleepless nights ensued as I replayed the key scenes of *North Wind* in my mind on the ceiling of my bedroom, lying awake, eyes wide open.

Chapter 20

Upsizing

April 11, 2001. American Express called wanting to know when they should expect to receive my past due payment (answer: "the check is in the mail"). Tony Heffner from the Hollywood management firm of Michael Levy Enterprises called to request copies of both *Scattered Seeds* and *CATV*, which represented my first response from sending 75 query letters to literary managers and agents the week before, drawn from the new 2001 directory of agents and managers. Darrah called to discuss Andy's plans for the upcoming Easter weekend—a T-ball game, a friend's birthday party, and an Easter egg hunt were on the schedule. With the divorce final now, all our energies focused on him. And I received a call from The Mulling Companies accepting my counter-offer to begin a full-time job with them in a sales/marketing capacity for their human resource consulting firm. It was a good day.

During the months leading up to this new job offer, and what was to be the 12th employer of my 22-year career, I had been enjoying freelance marketing projects through my Viking Group agency. This gave me the flexibility to go on interviews, as well as to take pause to consider where I was going, where I wanted to go, and where I should be going. Other than maintaining a deep (or as friends would say, "deeply crazed") conviction that my screenplays would find commercial exposure, I asked myself some serious questions, hoping I could come up with some honest answers. Who was I? What values drove me? What was I really good at doing, and what was that "something" that could make a difference? What talent had God given to me that I wasn't using, or that needed new expression? What was His plan? I needed to connect with a mission and a purposeful profession, not just a job. That much I did know.

What of my original goal when I had pursued my Bachelor of Science degree in psychology with hopes of going to graduate school to get a Ph.D., and then beginning a career in business or private practice with a concentration in training, testing, and motivation? I didn't have the money to go to grad school then, but was there an avenue now?

I enjoyed the sales and marketing disciplines, though. The creativity, the results-oriented nature, the interaction with so many people on a team to make something happen—these exercised my core values and talents, I felt. After reading Hyrum Smith's book *What Matters Most* about connecting internal values with career mission, I was motivated to dig deeper.

What mattered most to me, in its base essence, was to inspire people. The marketing messages I developed sought to inspire people, otherwise the marketing campaign wouldn't work. If the team of people creating the marketing program was not inspired, nothing inspirational would come of it. Whenever I found myself being inspired, it immediately triggered a response deep inside me to go out and try to inspire others. I tried to play sports as an inspired athlete. I tried my best to inspire the best when I was an athletic coach for the kids. I had tried my best to include messages of inspiration in my scripts. Inspiration was a core value with me.

One may learn the ways to inspire, manage, and lead people by watching the best *and* the worst bosses. I had had a goodly dose of both in my career to that point. My 11 different jobs had been filled with inspirational mentors as well as gutless, manipulative, self-serving cowards who confused motion with action, substituted bullying for real leadership, and relied on the status quo rather than vision to guide them. This exposure to a great many management styles was one of the benefits of having been downsized so many times, as was my having managed departments of up to 51 people. Although I was never the perfect boss, I always tried to give my best efforts to those I supervised. My most rewarding days were spent successfully fostering an environment for my junior managers to become great leaders, as well as on occasions when my employees paid me the compliment to follow me to my next job or company.

I still laugh to this day as I replay in my mind the comments made by bosses, as well as some job interviewers, who would exclaim that my undergraduate degree in psychology was "useless in a business setting." Too bad for them, those people who punch a clock and fail to recognize the opportunity to inspire people, and to be inspired by others. It's not about managing a box of rocks. It's Psychology 101.

I took a step back and suddenly began to see my résumé in a different light. There was an unstated résumé within my résumé. The values I held dear were those which included managing and inspiring people so that they grew to appreciate a balanced life—vocationally, avocationally, spiritually, physically, emotionally, and socially. Sometimes to the irritation of my management, I made these "non-job" goals a part of my employee's formal performance appraisal: I simply created my own forms and stapled them to the corporate review form. As a boss, I tried to establish an atmosphere of professional development, intellectual curiosity, and creative self-expression—all with a sense of humor: at least that's what my subordinates reported on *their* evaluations of me. It's amazing how much passion people can bring to their jobs when they don't feel they have to confine passion to other parts of their lives. Passion is contagious, and I was fortunate to be a "receiver" as much as I was a "giver" from employees and co-workers.

I had been downsized seven times in my career by companies ranging in size from small family-owned enterprises to multinational conglomerates. There were unstated lessons here, too. Values such as courage, resilience, and endurance came into play—values I was fortunate enough to learn from Mom and Dad, clergy, school teachers, and athletic coaches. When tough times come, as they do for everyone, habits are revealed, and trying to maintain balance and a balanced perspective come into play. That's why athletes practice so much: habit formation. I had shared these lessons with many downsized people on the unemployment line, and they empathized with me, those many times. We inspired each other.

What kind of job or industry was out there that would put my full experience to work? A job where inspiration was valued, where trust and sharing weren't just words written on a plaque hanging in the lobby, or a throw-away line in the annual report, where my experiences in a downsizing crisis would help someone, and where "balance" was not only valued but taught?

While these things played on my mind, I began studying the renaissance of a movement called "personal and executive coaching." Not a physical fitness fad, this "coaching" was the program in which a "coach" (counselor) helped people, alone or in a group, achieve stated goals by maximizing their talents, removing the obstacles that blocked their way to success, and by encouraging a fully balanced life. Not to be confused with "psychological therapy" or mere motivational pep talks, coaching brought accomplished people to even higher levels of achievement, effectiveness, and efficiency—demonstrably and quantifiably. Techniques such as the so-called "360" or "full circle" joint evaluations of a boss by the boss' superiors, the boss' peers, and the boss' subordinates, were changing the dynamic in the workplace by holding everyone accountable for mutual success; simply having all parties anonymously submit a list of the boss' good and bad behaviors could start the 360 process.

Also at this time, my own one-man Viking Group, Inc. was partnering with Tracy Arsenault of TAG Associates. Tracy and I had met and struck up a friendship years before, and I was overjoyed when she asked me to help with some sweepstakes promotions for a client of hers. After I shared with her the new direction I wanted to explore in my career, she suggested that I speak with another possible client of hers in Atlanta, The Mulling Companies, a 15-year old human resource consultancy firm which specialized in organizational assessment, outplacement management, and leadership development.

After introductions with The Mulling Companies' officers, I took the Birkman psychological test for them, with results that confirmed my strong social orientation and a good "salesmanship" profile. My creativity scores were also high, and when I frankly disclosed my passion for screenwriting, they thought it was very cool. I had found a home.

The testing also revealed that my organizational skills were better than those of 99% of the population, the highest they had seen. When this was reported to me, I had a brief, painful, yet humorous flashback to a boss I once had who told me that my organizational skills were getting in the way of my work! Not surprisingly, this boss had trouble locating stuff, which actually did get in the way of work.

Mulling's initial plan for me was to start in Business Development and Sales/Marketing, with some limited responsibility for empathetic employee outplacement counseling given at the time an employee is forced to leave a job, and then for me to eventually move into business coaching. Importantly, they wanted to first expand their human resource services and products to complement and enhance their current practice, and needed people with broad business experiences to accomplish that. I was undaunted that the current roster of long-time accounts was already assigned to other sales people, and that in addition to marketing assignments (which I was expected to do for free), I was supposed to develop (i.e., sales) a profitable client list from scratch (and on commission).

But, I was out there, running again.

✳✳✳

Air Force Colonel John Warden was a Vietnam pilot who was later responsible for developing the revolutionary attack plan for the swift victory in the Gulf War. John had translated his principles of military strategy to the business world when my Mulling Companies colleague Erik Lunkenheimer met John and struck a business alliance with him.

When I mentioned my screenwriting pursuits to John, he graciously offered to use his connections to screenwriter Eddie Neumeier whose *Starship Trooper* and *Robocop* were directed by Paul Verhoeven, also responsible for *Hollow Man, Showgirls, Basic Instinct,* and *Total Recall,* to name a few. John decided to send *North Wind* and *Scattered Seeds* to both Neumeier and Verhoeven as a favor to me. In the end, no responses.

✳✳✳

Terry Cunningham told me the results of the screenwriting competition conducted by Skorpeonyx Entertainment had been posted on the Internet. While the producer chose not to produce any of the 323 scripts submitted, *Scattered Seeds* was one of 15 listed on their web site for "special recognition." While my e-mail address was listed next to the script title on the web, no one ever inquired. But, it was another award.

✳✳✳

In early June, I received an e-mail from *Fade In Magazine.* In association with The Writer's Network, they were soliciting screenwriters to sign up for the Fifth Annual Hollywood Pitch Festival.

The Writer's Network was the group that had awarded both *Wheels* and *North Wind* quarter-finalist awards in their screenwriting competition in 1997.

The Pitch Festival was just that: a chance for screenwriters to pitch their scripts to "over 100 of Hollywood's top agents, managers, producers, and development executives." The event was to last about 10 hours per day, Saturday and Sunday, August 4th and 5th. Pitches were held to a maximum of seven minutes each. A short one-hour class on "how to pitch" preceded the event on the first morning. The Festival was limited to the first 200 applicants.

Before I reached a decision to attend the Festival, my conscience wrestled with itself a while:

ME: You can't afford to do this financially.
OTHER ME: It's not an expense, it's an investment.
ME: It's a huge waste of money. Money you don't have.
OTHER ME: Ah, no, I'm putting it all on a credit card.
ME: … which is almost maxed out.

I was hooked. I was in. I was going to LA!

Cost of Festival registration and a three-night stay at the Wyndham Bel Age in West Hollywood totaled $910.00, while the round-trip flight was free thanks to my frequent flier miles. I planned to fly in on Friday, and out on Monday. The dress code, the event planner told me on the phone, was suits for the studio executives, and golf shirts for writers.

***

I informed Fr. Eddie at Loyola Productions of my trip, and he quickly replied with an invitation to dinner to give me an update on his continued interest in and progress with *North Wind*. He signed his note with a resounding "There's hope!"

***

A night later, I had a dream. I was in the passenger seat of a biplane piloted by a leather-helmeted Robert Redford. The plane was either the one he flew in *The Great Waldo Pepper*, or the one in *Out of Africa*; I couldn't tell. Anyway, he circled the parking lot of the upcoming Pitch Festival hotel, and I tossed synopses from the plane upon the unsuspecting movie producers below.

I woke up laughing.

✳✳✳

When I was working for Turner Broadcasting in the early 1990s, a young Rhett Turner, son of Ted, was a management trainee. I remember spending some time with him as he roamed from department to department, learning all he could as fast as he could. He was a very sharp guy.

I also remember briefly, but not so subtly, mentioning my screenwriting pursuits. When news reports in mid-June told of how father Ted was forming Ted Turner Pictures in Atlanta, with Rhett as a producer, and the Civil War a primary interest, I decided to reintroduce myself. I tracked down his address, and sent an overnight package containing synopses of *Scattered Seeds*, *Wheels*, and Senator Max Cleland's letter of endorsement.

They didn't remain in business long enough for me to get a response.

✳✳✳

Change is a constant in any business, and certainly true in the development departments of film companies large and small. Development executives move on to be bigger development executives, or agents, or managers, or producers, or screenwriters, or something else. *Wheels*, *Scattered Seeds*, and *North Wind* were all rejected by Zide Entertainment in July, 2000, but a year later, a different development executive there at the renamed Zide/Perry, Marc Hernandez, requested *Wheels* the day before the Fourth of July. The request came as a result of my previous September's 5th place finish in the American Screenwriters Association competition. This award apparently made them rethink their previous rejection.

***

Fr. Eddie from Loyola Productions called on July 20 to ask me if he could put the synopsis of *North Wind* on the "projects under development seeking co-production help" section of his web site. I said sure, with many thanks. He also sent regrets that he wouldn't be able to meet me for dinner when I was in LA for Pitch Fest, because of his vacation plans. To Hawaii. I sent him $50 for sunscreen.

He did pledge that his VP of Development, Sharal Churchill, would try to meet me for dinner. My hope was to get any last-minute updates from her before heading into the pitches. Would Loyola seek a co-producer for *North Wind*? Could I help them locate one?

Within a couple days, I received a call from Sharal, confirming dinner for Friday night, August 3. She had an impressive bi-ography which was posted on their web site. As the former head of music for MGM, she served as film music supervisor for *The Substitute, Blue Sky, Little Women, Swimming with Sharks,* and *The Arrival.*

***

The weekend before Pitch Fest, I agonized for hours over the list of attending producers and agents. A participant was able to choose, and would be guaranteed, seven-minute pitches with only 12 people from a very large list of executives. After that, there was a first-come, first-served lottery format, which I didn't fully un-derstand, that would allow for subsequent meetings during the weekend.

The selection of the first dozen took on added importance. Two large agencies, International Creative Management and United Talent Agency, were at the top of my list, since they typi-cally don't accept solicitation mail or phone calls from first-tim-ers. Based on the written listing I received of what each producer sought (e.g., comedy, drama, etc.), I also tried to build a mix of

Wheels and *North Wind* into my first twelve. My only other planned pitch was *CATV* to former President of Paramount, Robert Evans, whose new company was looking for a political drama.

✳✳✳

A few days before the Pitch Festival, I received a postcard with a cool picture of the Farmers Market in LA, postmarked Marina Del Rey, from Terry Porter, with the message: "Call me, Brad. New things going on, and could have financing for your project."

Which project? *North Wind? Wheels? Scattered Seeds?* He had pitched them all at one time or another. I would soon find out.

Chapter 21

LA Diary

As I wrote this chapter, I glanced at the exercise diary I have kept for years. The dates August 3, 4, 5, and 6, 2001, are listed as "off days," which makes me smile as I think of how those days caused my heart to race as no exercise bout had in memory.

***

9:54 a.m., LA time, Friday, August 3. Plane lands at LAX. There is an expression in Hollywoodland that if someone is in LA, they are said to be "in town," versus anywhere else in the world, in which case they are "out of town." I was in town.

The taxi ride from the airport to the Pitch Fest host hotel, the Wyndham Bel Age in North Hollywood, crossed many of the streets to which I had addressed hundreds of query letters to producers and agents over the years. It was 80 degrees and sunny.

11:01 a.m. Check-in. Called Sharal Churchill at Loyola Productions to confirm dinner at 5 p.m. Then, I had lunch at the hotel restaurant ($12 for a salad!). Back to room to practice pitching and make some business calls.

4:35 p.m. Sharal calls from the lobby to report that she was going to meet an agent from Creative Artists Agency to receive some scripts, but he canceled. Further, she has to go to a screening at Paramount later, so all we have time for is coffee. We met in the lobby, and walked around the corner of Sunset Blvd. to a coffee shop. Two iced teas, my treat. I immediately find her to be warm, genuine, professional, endearing, and funny. She reports that she and Fr. Eddie are making the rounds of financiers and studios, and will continue to do so with top agencies International Creative Management and AEI Management; therefore, to eliminate confusion, I should not meet with those agencies at Pitch Fest. Before leaving, she reviews my one-pager of all my script log lines, and requests copies of *Wheels* and *Scattered Seeds*, which I will mail to her on my return to Atlanta. It's still 80 degrees and sunny.

6:11 p.m. Dinner at hotel.

7:30 p.m. With my body clock now telling me it's really 10:30 p.m., it's lights out.

6:00 a.m., Saturday. Wake-up call. Shave, shower, raid the in-room refrigerator for Oreos, water, and a can of Coke. The hotel restaurant is not yet open, but Pitch Fest registration is nearing. Putting on my shirt, I feel some of those "pregame jitters" one associates with playing sports. I was running in the open field again. It felt good. Stepping out onto the balcony of my room, I suck in a deep breath of (polluted?) air. It's 80 degrees and sunny.

7:00 a.m., registration. My typewritten, prepared sticker name tag reads "brad catherman, atlanta, ga" in all lower-case letters. Very chic. Very LA. We are handed a timesheet with 12 blank spaces on which we write the names of the producer/agent companies with whom we will meet, and then are ushered into the large ballroom. On the left side are tables with the Sunday meetings sign-up sheets, and on the right side, the Saturday meetings. We are given one hour to make the rounds of all the tables and sign up on the producer/agents' time logs, which are taped to the table. We then make the corresponding notations on our own personal timesheet which we will keep and have initialed by the administrator prior to each meeting.

There is some strategy involved with this: referring to my previous notes on the producers whose needs matched my scripts, I had to race around the tables, while everyone else was racing around the tables, to find time slots which did not conflict with one another. The other problem was that some companies canceled their appearance, while others were added, which ruined my pregame plan a little—but gave me time to make some open field moves on the fly. I completed the task, and had 10 of my 12 slots completed. We were informed that any remaining slots on our timesheets could be filled on a first-come, first-served basis by standing in a line outside the door at the beginning of each session—if there was a vacancy.

The format was explained as follows: the pitches would last 5 minutes each, with about two minutes of time for the changing of each session, and run 9 hours a day for the two days. At the 3-minute mark, a bell would sound, and an official would walk around and tap the writer on the shoulder; a minute later, another bell would sound the end of the session, and the writers would leave the ballroom while the next batch of 20 or so writers would enter and find their places. My first meeting was at 9 a.m. Saturday, thus I would miss the "how-to-pitch-a-script class" (forfeiting my prepaid $30); I didn't meet any other writer who took this class, so I never learned what I missed.

9:04 a.m. First pitch session of the conference. They are starting a little late, and would run a few minutes late throughout the weekend. I was first in line, had my first time slot initialed by the official guarding the door, and was the first one through the door of the ballroom. Like the annual running of the bulls in Spain, the crush behind me is intense as we fan out to try to find the alphabetical listing of our target. My first 5-minute session was with Fred Lidscog of Konrad Pictures (*Scream 1, 2,* and *3, Cop Land,* and *Girl, Interrupted*); the booklet said they were looking for "anything except horror," and that they had a production deal with Columbia. I pitched *Wheels,* and Fred laughed out loud, and was still smiling when I left the table. Being a little wound up, I almost jumped out of my chair when the conference woman lightly tapped me on the shoulder at the 2-minute warning. While Fred didn't ask me to send him a script, I saw him writing some notes as I left the room. Good sign, I guessed. Maybe he might call me later? (And was that a nervous writer who suddenly threw up on the other side of the room? I hoped I didn't have to attend a meeting over in that direction.)

9:58 a.m. Pitched *North Wind* to Marc Roskin, Jeff Smith, and another woman executive whose name I didn't catch. They were from Electric Entertainment (*Independence Day, The Patriot, Stargate*), and looking for "a Big Major Event, but no Romantic/Comedy." At the end, Marc (or was it Jeff?) said "Sounds interesting …" but no request came my way to send them a script or synopsis. I was beginning to get a rhythm of the meetings, however, and my internal clock was learning to live in 5-minute space. The tap on the shoulder in the pitches which followed helped me immensely to know where I was, and how to short-cut to the end of my pitch. I was so engrossed in my pitch, and the responses coming from the other side of the table, that along with the general conversational noise level in the large ballroom, I seldom heard the warning bell.

10:24 a.m. Pitched *CATV* to Sam Dowde-Sandes at Robert Evans Company. Their need for a "Thriller/Drama" sent me into the telling of my political murder mystery. Sam asked for a written synopsis, although we were told that executives wouldn't/shouldn't do that at the session; but executives asked and all writers, including myself, were ready to oblige. I handed him a one-page synopsis of *CATV* as well as a one-pager of all my script log lines. It had been 18 years at that point since I had written my first draft of *CATV*.

10:48 a.m. Breakfast—or was it brunch? What time was it back east? Was I hungry or not? I had scrambled eggs and fruit, which just about covered every meal. Back to my room to practice pitching in the mirror.

3:29 p.m. Pitched *Wheels* to Josh Markman of Mike Lobell Productions (*Honeymoon in Vegas, Striptease, It Can Happen To You, White Fang*), which had a deal with Castle Rock. His response: "Gee, I really think it would be hard to find an actor or actress who would sit in a wheelchair for the whole movie ..." Early exit.

5:23 p.m. It's 80 degrees and sunny as I walk to a sandwich shop on Sunset Boulevard, then to a cigar store to get my favorite brand—Fuente—in stock, fortunately.

6:00 p.m. Pro football exhibition game on TV between the Dallas Cowboys and the Oakland Raiders.

9:05 p.m. Asleep.

7:30 a.m. Sunday. Wake-up call, and I bound out of bed anticipating another exciting day! Was I jet-lagged? Did jet lag go from east to west, or west to east? Did the fact that I slept 10 hours nullify the difference? It was 80 degrees and sunny outside when I went downstairs for breakfast.

9:21 a.m. I called Mom in Atlanta. The previous week had marked the third anniversary of Dad's death, and as the phone rang and rang and rang (Mom didn't like answering machines), I was lost in thought and half expected Dad to answer the phone. Mom told me that her Sunday School Class was into overtime prayers for me. She asked me about the weather, and I replied that it's generally 80 degrees and sunny.

10:20 a.m. I was to meet David Boxerbaum from RKO Pictures (*Mighty Joe Young, Magnificent Ambersons*) and pitch *North Wind*, but the RKO meetings had time-shifted 6 hours. I was now on with him at 4:20 p.m. Fortunately, I had nothing scheduled at 4:20 p.m. So, back to the room for more Oreos and practice.

12:15 p.m. Pitched *North Wind* to Rachel Katz of Persistent Pictures (*Auggie Rose, Stand Off*) which claimed to have $50 million to spend on a big-event, "Opening Weekend Picture." I had a good pitch, and she requested and received a one-page synopsis of *North Wind* and a one-pager of all my log lines. As I exited the room, I glanced back and saw she was still reading my log lines page. Good sign.

1:05 p.m. Pitched *North Wind* to Susan Hirschberg of Morgan Creek (*Ace Ventura, Robin Hood, Young Guns, Major League*). She politely cut me off, saying that they were about to hire a director for their own Viking movie entitled *Northmen.* Ouch! Their story was much different, though. They were about "two years" away from a target completion date. Silence. The warning bell rang. I heard it this time. How about a Civil War movie? Sure, she said! I pitched *Scattered Seeds* in the remaining minute, and she asked for a synopsis on the spot: I obliged with a two-page synopsis, and my one-page log lines of all my scripts.

1:20 p.m. Pitched *North Wind* to Stephen Gilchrist from Canton Pictures (*Red Planet, Angel Eyes*). They had a development deal with Warner Brothers, and were a late entry to the festival. I was asked for a synopsis at the table, and handed over the synopsis of that, and logs of my other scripts.

1:31 p.m. Free buffet of fruit, salad, Mexican fixings, and dessert. There wasn't much chatting going on, but the expressions on the faces spoke volumes about the internal discussions going on: how many scripts had been requested? did I remember to explain the plot clearly? were my characters any good? is there any dessert left?

I sat next to a guy who looked as if he had been beaten up— literally. He had. The night before Pitch Fest, he and some pals had been drinking until 3 a.m., and he was walking alone back to the hotel when he was beaten and robbed. His black eye and chipped front teeth were the result. He remained philosophical, however, knowing that the trip back to Colorado would be more pleasant if he sold a screenplay this weekend.

4:20 p.m. I gave my best and most upbeat pitch of the weekend to Caleigh Vancata of Tollin/Robbins (*Smallville, Varsity Blues*), which had a deal with Warner Brothers. I pitched *Wheels*, and she immediately requested a synopsis. When I also handed her my one-pager of log lines, she read intently, then looked up and said, "Atlanta? You came all the way here for this? You're ambitious!" I thanked her. Upon leaving, she said she would call me, and when she would, she might ask for other scripts, pointing to *Brothers' Brunch* and *Wings on High* on my log sheet. I stuttered another "thank you," and bumped into the next writer to sit in that chair.

4:50 p.m. The Saturday "10:20 a.m." slot for RKO, now scheduled for 4:20 p.m. today, was about to begin, the festival now 30 minutes behind schedule. Except RKO never showed. So, I asked the official in charge of scheduling if he could find me an agent or manager left inside the ballroom. A new afternoon replacement, he walked me over to management company FourSight Entertainment Group, and its manager, George Heller. George told me that they were looking for "anything good," so I asked permission to pitch *Wheels*, a romantic comedy. He nodded, and I launched into it. Upon my completion, he handed me a raised letter business card and asked me to send him the full-length script. Touchdown!

I was later to learn that George, a fast-tracker from the renowned University of Southern California film school, was only 23 years old. He was 15 years old when I wrote *Wheels*.

5:10 p.m. Pitched *North Wind* to Ms. Max Wong of indy Pink Slip (*Bring It On, Tuck Everlasting*), looking to spend up to $100 million on a "High End Genre Movie." She volunteered halfway through my pitch that they were "working on something similar." "How about Civil War"? I asked. "No, actually harder to make and distribute." The bell. "Comedy?" I begged in a last-ditch effort. "I liked your Viking script," she said. "You should take it to Mel Gibson at Icon." Final bell.

I kept close watch on the availability of my targeted producers and agents, but due to a conflict of scheduling, or a cancellation, or having a full schedule, I couldn't manage more than 10 meetings over the weekend.

5:30 p.m. Italian Sub shop on Sunset Blvd. for a light dinner and post-game reflections.

6:13 p.m. Balcony of my hotel room, to the left the Hollywood hills and those houses which look like they might slide off at any minute, to the right a view of downtown. Good cigar and cold beer from the in-room refrigerator. Engulfed in thought. Satisfied, mostly. Wondering if the effort would bring more requests for scripts. Reaching in my pocket and gently rubbing the raised letter business card from that manager. Would I ever sell anything?

Looking skyward now, squinting, and smiling. It was 80 degrees and sunny.

Chapter 22

LA Revisited

By Wednesday of the week following pitch fest, I had not received any phone calls. Or letters. Or e-mails. During the 10 pitches, I had handed out six requested synopses, and upon my return I'd sent a script to FourSight via FedEx. So, on Wednesday night, while Andy was occupied by crawling on his tummy in his darkened room, with a flashlight, wearing his football helmet, "looking for a leprechaun for good luck" under his bed and in the closets, I took the quiet moment to send a follow-up letter to Sam Dowe-Sandes at Robert Evans Company. Sam received his synopsis of *CATV* at the event, but I thought I would keep up his interest in the script by sending him a batch of 20-year old press clippings about corruption and FBI convictions in the 1980s-era cable television industry.

Likewise, since I had not received that phone call from Caleigh Vancata at Tollin/Robbins as she had hinted I might, I sent her a letter of thanks along with a copy of my *Symbol Magazine* bio/ article.

But whatever came of Pitch Fest, at least I had connected with Loyola Productions, face to face. That alone was worth the trip.

✳✳✳

I don't like computers. I don't like hardware, software, or the frustrationware that comes with them. Usually, I find myself on the "help line" of some computer company giving them my creditcardware to pay *them* to help me use *their* stuff.

After a few years of procrastination, I decided to use my now-heightened optimismware about my chances of selling a screenplay to upgrade my screenwriting software. This entailed converting all my scripts to new software which would make it theoretically easier to revise them in the rewrite stages.

I went line by line, script by script. It only took about 70 hours of work and gave me "mouse elbow" from moving the page margins around.

✳✳✳

I continued to send scripts to all possible leads. The July 10, 2001, issue of *The Hollywood Reporter* carried an ad for AS Productions—"seeking treatments." I sent several, and on August 14 received a call at home from Victoria Prismantas of their development group wanting the full-length *North Wind* and *Scattered Seeds* scripts. AS Productions was a unit of The American Sterling Group, a company with interests in banking, insurance, and mortgage loan development. They had recently gone into the motion picture business of all things, and produced their first film entitled *The Annihilation of Fish*, starring Lynn Redgrave, James Earl Jones, and Margot Kidder. Their web site invited synopses, and I e-mailed all my synopses in mid-August.

Was this finally to be my big break? Could they buy a script and also get me a great mortgage rate?

✳✳✳

On October 8, 2001, I received a rejection of *Wheels* from the production company Graham/Rosenzweig (*Act Normal*). They had requested the two-page synopsis in December of 2000—a waiting period of ten *months* to read and respond to two pages. They never read the full script.

✳✳✳

Ran across a web site claiming that the film financier to Hilton Head's Straw Hut (aka Strawhut, which had optioned *North Wind* and claimed that "money was king"), one Marlene Mendoza, had filed bankruptcy and was *"a fraud . . . "*

✳✳✳

The fire alarm sounded at my apartment in the middle of a night when Andy was staying with me: it is said that one can truly gauge a person's value system by watching people scurry out of a building during a fire, and see what they are carrying. I grabbed Andy, my screenplay computer discs (and the one for this book), car keys, and my wallet, and fled. It turned out to be a false alarm.

✳✳✳

On Halloween night, 2001, I received an e-mail reply from George Heller at FourSight Entertainment—whom I had met at Pitch Fest. I had sent George an e-mail saying (half untruthfully) that I had some interest in *Wheels* from an Atlanta investor group, and needed to know if he shared that interest.

His e-mail reply: "Regrettably, the project does not match our sensibilities."

Huh?

Chapter 23

The Journey

The November 3, 2001, front page of *The Atlanta Journal* screamed "Job Losses Skyrocket." The recession, fueled in part by the tragic events of September 11, contributed to the fact that "more Americans lost their jobs in October than in any other month in the last 21 years ..." A few days later, having spent just six months with The Mulling Companies, I was dismissed by the Chairman, adding my own statistic to the headline.

My direct boss, the president of my division, had been let go the week before. Others in sales had quit ahead of him to pursue other opportunities, sensing correctly that the "new products and services" which were to be introduced would take too long to bring to market, and didn't really fit the strategy of the company. Mulling didn't want to invest any more time or marketing money into new programs, wishing instead to get back to their core businesses. They realized they wouldn't be successful straying from their competencies and base of contacts. The experiment was over.

My own path with the company had been a frustrating one. It was tough to start without a roster of billing clients, all previously assigned to the existing sales people, and to crack companies already knee deep into competitors' programs and long-term contractual relationships. Moreover, the non-sales (i.e., uncompensated) marketing assignments I was saddled with took away from my commissioned sales time, all the while I was trying to help grow the company and be a team player, helping to lay the groundwork for the future. In the end, I felt used.

The largest potential sales deal I pursued, which was canceled by an oil client who felt the effects of the recession, would have paid me over $300,000 in commission plus coaching fees for the first 18 month consulting assignment. I never surpassed my sales commission draw, but if Mulling had paid me a typical hourly rate based on my experience just for my marketing management efforts, they would have owed me more than my draw.

My severance package, from a company that specialized in outplacement empathy (ahem), was $00.00. And I was not even offered a complimentary trip through the company's own job search outplacement program!

Could I have seen it coming? Unlike the mergers and acquisitions in past downsizings, which caught me totally off-guard, this was a little different. When the division president told us that it would take two years to get the new products and services into the marketplace, and then asked, "What have you done for me lately?" only six *months* later, who's to blame? It was their football and their rules: one either made the choice to trust or not to trust at the beginning of employment. I was trusting. Too trusting? Or was I naive?

However, the Chairman, Emory Mulling, did invite me to submit a proposal on how to promote and sell his new business book, which was to be published a few months later. Ironically, the subject of the book was the value of bringing together boss and employee in a business environment that yielded maximum effectiveness. I wasn't hired to do the marketing project.

Elsewhere in the news at that time was a similar situation at a loftier level: Ted Turner himself was "continuing" to be downsized by AOL/Time Warner, his responsibilities eroding, little by little, like being eaten alive. No one was immune, but Ted's "severance check" was bigger than mine.

A bizarre ending: after I had departed The Mulling Companies, without any communication from the firm for many months, Emory Mulling sent a letter to former sales people "requesting" that we *return our draw* paid during the time we worked for the company, even though we were under no legal obligation to do so! This from a human resources company?

I had seldom felt as hurt or offended at any other time in my two decades in the business world. Request denied.

✳✳✳

So, my journey took me back to the unemployment office. For the eighth time. During the previous six months a new carpet and a new online registration system had been installed, and the weekly payment had increased $10, to $284 before tax. I was at the bottom of a mountain of debt. Instead of electing to have taxes deducted, I asked for the full weekly amount.

And then, when the weight of stress seemed unbearable, Andy gave me a smile, and reminded me about the gift of him, when he came up with this at bedtime that night:

ANDY: Dad, read that Bible story about how Jesus made 5000 grilled cheese sandwiches from only one loaf of bread!

✳✳✳

The next day, I received an e-mail from Marita Ekman, the Editor of *Viking Heritage* magazine in Sweden, accepting my letter-to-the-editor asking their readership if they knew of any Hollywood contacts who may be interested in a Viking screenplay. At that time in 2001, the magazine enjoyed distribution to subscribers in 27 countries around the world.

I never received a response from anyone, anywhere.

✳✳✳

That same week, Keith Finger, whom I had met at the state unemployment office years before and who introduced me to the movie-making-dentist, tracked me down after five years to say hello and to do some career networking of his own. I told him what I had been going through that week and for the past few years, and he urged me to take heart, saying that after the five downsizings he had been through, he finally learned that "he" was not his circumstances. He refused to consider his inner-self to be synonymous with his résumé, or what "someone in power" thought. Keith had turned to a personal coach during the previous year to help him become stronger and more confident. Also, he was blessed, he said, with a wife who also was able to separate "him" from his "circumstances," and who loved him for better or worse, richer or poorer. They had two great kids.

He encouraged me to keep the faith, trust myself, and continue to move in the direction of my dreams: look forward, not backward.

✳✳✳

The November/December, 2001 issue of *Script* magazine quoted Chuck Konzelman and Cary Solomon of Numenorean Films as saying, "We want the dented cans out there—the guys who have been beaten to a pulp—to come to us and let us do the hard work for them. We want to build long-term relationships with talented people."

The article went on to say that Numenorean received 12,000 queries *a year* and read 5,000 to 6,000 of them (plus an unstated number of full-length screenplays requested in response to queries), but only chose three or four of them for filming. They had film productions in the works with cumulative budgets in excess of $100 million, in a distribution pipeline in over 80 countries. Their upcoming film was an adaption of Troon McAllister's award-winning novel *The Green*, which would star Sylvester Stallone.

I liked my chances, though, and sent them a letter. No one was as dented as me.

✳✳✳

November 13, 2001—I sent an e-mail to Fr. Eddie and Sharal at Loyola Productions proposing that they buy *North Wind* for

$500,000. I offered easy payment terms: $10 a year for 50,000 years unless the movie went into production before the end of the payment period, at which time they would owe me the balance immediately.

How could they refuse a great deal like that? Publicity would be immense, right?

***

On Thanksgiving night, I received an e-mail from Numenorean Films, the guys looking for the "dented cans." They requested both *North Wind* and *Scattered Seeds*. I was thankful. Although they later passed on both, they said they liked my writing talent and that their "door was always open" to me to submit future scripts.

***

I always had a plan. And another one after that one. Always planning ahead. But what was God's plan for me and my writing? His Will? I had never been a patient person, and may never be. But after 18 years of trying to improve my writing craft to achieve commercial success, I had learned two things: God had answered my prayers to help me find at least *some* patience necessary to continue, and that the gift of writing that God had revealed to me was a joy in itself, even without commercial success.

At the very least, my journey had been filled with the pleasure of creating, and the lesson of patience that was necessary to fuel this passion. Sure, who wouldn't want to see their script on the screen? But, how could one achieve success without passion and patience? Whether commercial success was to ever be mine, the pain of rejections which felt like daggers through the heart subsided quicker and quicker as time went by.

With passion and patience by my side, the hard part was over. But would commercial success ever follow?

Chapter 24

Coming Soon
to a Theatre Near You

I have a poem hanging on a wall at home. My Dad had it hanging on his wall for many years, from his college days on. It's entitled *Achievement*, and goes:

Who says that the day of Achievement is gone?
'Twas never more certainly Here!
The summons to Youth "Carry On! Carry On!"
Was never so urgent and clear!
Today calls for youth self-reliant and true,
Courageous, clear-visioned and free —
Who fashion a program and carry it through
Whatever its problems may be.
Today offers you greater honor and fame
Than history has ever known,
And uncounted millions will herald your name
The moment your merit is shown!

The poem meant different things to me at different times in my life. When I was still a competitive athlete, the poem's promise to me was that I could gain great fame and glory on a ball field as a professional athlete. Millions would watch and cheer. I clung to that poem for decades after those dreams had died, but sometimes I was puzzled by it, and once I actually put it into a drawer because I thought it irrelevant. Actually, too painful to see. Then I took up screenwriting, which while rewarding in its own right, also held the promise of admiration from millions and millions of people.

Mom, my brother Gary, and I stood by the side of my Dad's hospital bed on the early morning of July 23, 1998 and watched him slip into Heaven, leaving behind the pain of cancer. Dad would have been 71 years old just three days later. Dad had gone from perfect health to this hospital bed in just two months. After surviving cancer some 25 years before, in the next three days as I planned the eulogy I was to deliver at the church service, I reflected upon his life, and in so doing, came to an understanding and appreciation of my own place in life.

My eulogy, which was audiotaped for friends and relatives who couldn't attend, lasted 30 minutes. I told a few stories about Dad which illustrated the love he had for life, and his tireless efforts to help young people, including my brother and myself: the time he saved a kid from drowning; the many times he taught me how to handle adversity with patience and hard work; the time he taught another kid how to throw a football, which would one day pay off for that kid with a college scholarship to play quarterback at the University of Georgia; his stint as a Boy Scout leader, helping young boys become young men by learning the meaning of "Be Prepared."

Dad had a sense of history, and his place in it. His father, my Grampa, was a Methodist minister in small towns all over eastern Pennsylvania. I remarked during the eulogy that I still carried Grampa's ring in my pocket for good luck—the luck which comes from my Grampa having worn the ring while giving thousands of sermons from pulpits just like the one in which I stood. Our family tree was blessed with some sharp and dedicated genealogists who had researched the current 10 generations of our line since coming from Germany (and before Germany, who knows, perhaps Viking-land!). Dad and I used to read the genealogy book together, and he would share stories with me about people from generations past whom he knew, or knew of. There, in their workshops, or on their farms, or by their fishing ponds, I could imagine fathers teaching sons about patience, hard work, and love of life just as Dad had taught me. Lessons which endure from generation to generation.

I spoke of Dad's "moments of truth"—moments that defined his personality, and moments that let others catch a glimpse of what was residing deep inside of him. Stories like the one about the time he walked back to the counter of a McDonald's restaurant and gave back $5 to the kid behind the counter because Dad was given too much change. Or, stories about the time he saved that drowning boy. Or, stories about the time I witnessed him miraculously snagging a jumping fish by the tail and reeling it in backwards (!), only to let the fish go because "it wasn't sportsmanship to catch and keep a fish in that way ... and patience needs to be rewarded by catching a fish the right way."

Dad helped me prepare my weekly messages for Emory University's SAE Fraternity when I was elected Chaplain there, counseling me that rather than focusing on the "religious salvation" of my fellow students, I just ought to make sure no one went to jail or to the Dean's Office.

Stories about ... the many times he would coach me, or some other kid, or my son Andy, and repeat over and over again, "Keep your eye on the ball." As I have grown older, I have learned that "Keep your eye on the ball," in another sense of Dad's teaching, meant much more: find your talents and share them with others, stay focused on the task at hand and on the important things in life, teach lessons which can endure from generation to generation.

Because I was emotionally and physically drained, I had to skip some parts of the eulogy I had prepared. Standing there in front of about 150 people, each of whom had become a part of our family that day, and trying to do the very best I could to remember Dad, was the single hardest challenge I've ever faced. The service and the reception which followed were a blessing. We saw people whom we had not seen for a long time, and two of Dad's business associates, Dick Shockly and Jim Thrower, remarked that although they hadn't seen me for decades, I reminded them of Dad. I had his hands, they said.

Lots of people loved Dad and will miss him. We had many requests for the tape of the eulogy. Sportscaster Ernie Johnson, Sr. mentioned my Dad's passing on a televised Atlanta Braves' baseball game. Ernie, Sr. had played some golf with Dad, and Ernie, Jr., himself a sportscaster, and I went to Marist School together. A friend of my brother Gary's pledged a donation to the Passionists, an organization which calls aloud during a daily religious service the names of people who have passed away.

As if the events of the week of Dad's death weren't enough, Andy, then 3, had to be taken to the hospital emergency room a couple days before the memorial service because he had symptoms of what seemed like appendicitis. As I lay next to him on the narrow emergency room bed and looked into his bright blue eyes, offering him comfort, I remembered all the times through all the years when I had looked into Dad's deep blue eyes as he had comforted me. Andy checked out fine, and they sent us home about midnight.

It wasn't until after the eulogy, when I was going through some of Dad's old papers, that I remembered that poem entitled *Achievement*. My Dad had a profound and wonderful sense of history: he knew if "ordinary" people could positively influence the course of life of a single young person, a young person who was seeking guidance and leadership, and answers to life's tough questions, then this young person, upon growing up, could in turn influence the course of life of many other young persons, and so on, until what was being influenced was the course of history itself. The millions of people who have been influenced in such a positive way, not by the rich and famous but by ordinary people who take the time to give extraordinarily of themselves, combined with the millions of people yet to come who will benefit from these millions, are the "millions" in the poem. Help just one person along your way and you will influence millions, generation to generation.

✳✳✳

Andy was staying with me on my forty-sixth birthday, November 28th, 2001. That morning, I was treated to a small concert via voicemail by my college fraternity brother and Andy's godfather, Clyde Partin, and his son, as they played "Happy Birthday" with a horn instrument of some kind. Was it a trumpet? Bugle? French horn? Tuba? Even though the notes were a little crooked, it was a sweet, sweet, sound.

Andy promised to take me to McDonald's for dinner on my birthday, and we had a great time. The kid at the counter gave me too much change, and so I gave it back to him, of course, just as Dad had done.

At home that evening, it was the regular routine—a shower for Andy, homework, packing lunch for the next day at school, writing additions to Andy's Christmas Wish List, which was hanging on the refrigerator. I glanced at the TV and saw Director Joel Schumacher's name flash across the screen, which brought a smile to my face. One day I would tell Andy how I spoke with the director of *Batman*.

Later, Andy and I were playing cards (he was killing me, as usual) when the phone rang. I glanced at my watch with two faces: 7:30 p.m. East Coast time, 4:30 p.m. on the West Coast. It was Sharal Churchill from Loyola Productions. She had called to discuss my offer to sell *North Wind*. I had spoken with Fr. Eddie earlier in the day. He was upbeat as usual about the prospects of producing *North Wind*, and told me that Sharal would be calling during the evening to discuss specifics.

Sharal said that while they weren't in a position to offer any immediate payment except for a token dollar to make things legally binding, they wanted to buy the script with a pre-negotiated price in order to show studios and financiers that they controlled the script. Her offer was to pay me the *greater* amount of the Writers Guild minimum for a "high budget" film (defined as having a budget of $5 million or more), or half of one percent of the production cost, at such time that they would have a contract with a studio to make and distribute the film. In 2001, the WGA minimum payment for a screenwriter for a high budget film was $91,495.00, but the more likely scenario for me was half a percent of everyone's best-guess for the production cost of $50 million, which would pay me $250,000 before production could begin. Then she wished me a happy birthday.

After some 18 years since first starting on this journey, and although there was no immediate payment except for another dollar, I had contractually sold a screenplay. A hollow victory? Thousands of screenwriters would have gladly exchanged places with me. It was another step.

I missed Dad at times like this. Without thinking, one of my first reactions was to pick up the phone and call him with the good news. He always made you feel that news of your victories counted more to him than his own. But somehow, I could feel Dad's presence and pleasure in this moment. He knew. I did return my mom's call of birthday well-wishes, and told her the good news.

It was time for bed, and Andy was singing parts of the refrain sung by Jiminy Cricket in *Pinocchio*: "When you wish upon a star … when you wish upon a star … when you wish upon a star …" I helped Andy finish the verse. Dreams do come true.

I finished replying to some e-mails from friends, and thought of many others who had helped me get to where I was in the world over those 46 birthdays:

People who counted someone else's accomplishments above their own.

Friends who overcame time and distance to stay friends.

People who freely shared their own passion as a gift and an inspiration.

People who gave their time when it was more valuable than money.

People who gave me a chance.

People who gave me a second chance.

Like George Bailey in *It's a Wonderful Life*, I was the richest man in town.

And when the day was finally done, and the entire range of emotions had consumed me, I sat at the bottom of the bathtub as the shower poured over me, and cried. It felt good.

Chapter 25

A Christmas Story

On the drive to a holiday party a few days before Christmas in 2003, I was stopped at a red light. I put the car in park, and quickly reached into my pocket for some 3" x 5" index cards upon which I was continuing to outline a new screenplay. In moments when dialogue plays in one's head, you either write it down or it's gone for good. When the Muse visits, you can't turn her away. The driver behind me honked their horn when the light turned green as I was lost in thought, but I was able to capture most of it on the card before I had to move on. I was outlining two scripts at that time, one an idea for a contemporary remake of *Same Time, Next Year*, the 1978 romantic comedy starring Alan Alda and Ellen Burstyn. The other concept was semi-autobiographical about the high school senior year of four students at an all-boys military school during the Vietnam years.

At the next red light, I stopped and reflected about screenplays as a form of writing. Was a screenplay actually *literature*? A painter can paint a painting, and whether sold or not, have a completed art form to hang on a wall. A poem can be written and then read to oneself, or read aloud to a group of people, whether commerce was an aim or not. It's complete. But a screenplay with a big budget requires the talents of hundreds of people strung across the globe for its fruition.

But, can a screenplay be *literature* as simply *read* by audiences other than students who are in training to write more screenplays? Can the scenes, characters, dialogue, and action of a screenplay "play" in the ultimately creative arena in the world—that is, in the human imagination? If screenplays that had not been produced were published and purchased, would the *theatre of the mind* become another "channel" for their "viewing?" Could the reader be taught to use their imagination to supply their own camera angles to bring the script to life in the same way in which a reader supplies such mental imagery to a novel? In a world of instant downloads of filmed entertainment and interactive games of all stripes, can the person seeking diversion find that they can be their own Best Director Of Their Own Imagination with a screenplay in hand? Is training the mind's eye to produce a *mental* movie from a written screenplay, including mentally *casting* movie stars of one's own choosing, the same as producing *literature*?

On the drive to the party, I was also thinking about the Oscar trophy that the hostess said her mother won for acting. Would I get to see it? Was it locked up somewhere? Even though I had met the hostess only once—months before—through an Internet dating service, and hadn't seen her since, would I be imposing too much to ask to see it? Although we didn't have a second date, we became friends, and she did ask me to the party, after all. I had helped her brainstorm for a book proposal she was writing.

Could I hold it? Once? Was it really as heavy as people said?

I had taken a job the year before in the Advancement Department of Marist School in Atlanta, the private school where I graduated in 1974. The hundred-year-old predominantly Catholic school of grades 7 through 12 boasted a rich tradition in academics, community service, arts, athletics, spirituality, and other extracurricular activities. *Sports Illustrated* ranked the high school athletics program as being the 15th best in the *nation*. The Art History discipline was ranked the best program among schools in the *world*. My job entailed various aspects of marketing, fund raising, and (mostly) reliving days of athletic glory with alumni. I was having a blast. The southern region of the *Council for Advancement and Support of Education* bestowed their Award of Excellence for my marketing results. Being a single Dad to eight year-old Andy, I was also keen on exposing him to the school in hopes that it might be a place where he would want to attend.

At any gathering outside of school, I was a target of parents wanting to know how to get their kids into the school. The reality was that there were no secrets or back doors, although everyone kept trying. At the party, where I knew no one, conversations moved from how we all knew the hostess (to which I lied), to careers, to sports, and to how to get their kids or friends' kids into Marist School. Of course, I was always trying to steer the conversation to whom they may know in Hollywood—easier in that setting since the walls were filled with old movie posters of the hostess' mother, which provided a ready conversation starter.

I mingled about, enjoying the food and drink, admiring the season's decorations, and meeting other guests. Entering the den, and curious to see what was on the other side of the Christmas tree, I saw a golden glow from behind the tree—a light which appeared brighter than all the other lights in the room. Intrigued, I glanced around the other side, and there sat Oscar, alone on a table. The reflection of light in the room on the statue made the object appear to be the brightest light source of all.

I looked behind me, half expecting a security guard or someone to yell, "Hey you, don't touch that!" I indulged myself and picked it up. In a room packed with people, I was hidden, all alone, behind a Christmas tree, holding the Academy Award. Lights of all colors of the rainbow danced off it, the golden hue of Oscar the brightest color of all.

For the rest of the party, I was content to make trips back and forth to the hors d'oeuvre table, and then disappear again to pick up the Oscar. It was heavy. Did it ... vibrate a little?—or was that my imagination because I was so excited to hold it? Maybe it was the wine, and I was vibrating. Maybe a little of both.

I was intercepted on one of my trips back and forth to Oscar:

WOMAN: I hear you ... write? Stage plays? Cookbooks? What?

ME: I sold a Viking screenplay which will hopefully get funded soon.

WOMAN: Are you somebody yet?

ME: Well, no ...

WOMAN: Wait! Are you the one who works at Marist School?!

ME: Yes.

WOMAN: Oh, then you *are* somebody! I have a young niece who wants to enroll at Marist, and ...

And then back to the tree, and Oscar. To dream. To think. To hope. To make resolutions for the New Year. My mind drifted to the order forms for Hollywood agent and producer directories sitting in a mound on my coffee table at home. More queries to go out to start the new year, for sure. And then, my eyes drifted upward to the top of the tree, and to the bright star that was providing the light to make the Oscar glow in my hand. The source of the light was that Christmas star, not Oscar, and made me mindful that God, the source of all light, would go ahead of me to shine the way into another new year. What was His plan for me? I didn't have all the answers. I was content, however, that I had the right question to begin anew.

Chapter 26

Next!

There are a great many loose ends regarding some of the people and stories in this book. Some of the leads for future script sales were nothing but more of the many dead ends which confront me still. Some of the unfinished business here may never come to a conclusion, good or bad. The next time my phone rings, it could bring news of the beginning of production of *North Wind*. But creative business is the business of rejection, and a future unknown. It comes with the territory, as does the joy of creating for its own sake.

But this is as it should be. A career in screenwriting, or the momentum of any particular script, or a lead to a possible sale, doesn't run in straight lines, and neither does life. No, the running is in the open field, where one pushes for progress amidst the chaos. Some of the loose ends of this book might become the bright ribbons which wrap another prize, making the wait and work all worth it.

***

When one finds their passion—their gift—their talent—and seeks to share it with others, this has a way of energizing one's courage and endurance, which fuels hope. And with our hope, and God's power through prayer, all things are possible.

For all of the excitement which will come with the uncertainty, I can't wait until tomorrow. I'll be out there, somewhere, running in the open field again.

Come join me. Find your passion. Dream your dream. Exercise your talent. Then, make *your* dream come true!

9 781596 635678